"One thing seems abundan
answer to the challenges t
Allen Langham found, anyt
you down, but only one th
back up."

**Peter Wreford, editor-in-chief at New Life
Publishing**

"This is a story of transformation. Allen was addicted to
violence and drugs, and spent years in prison. By God's grace
he has found a path to freedom, peace, purpose, and hope.
His well-told story grabs the attention from the first page. If
you want evidence of the power of Christ to change, heal, and
redirect a man's life, you will find it here."

Tony Collins, editor and author

"There are three things that I love and share in common with
Allen Langham: Jesus Christ, fishing, and rugby league. I always
smile at the humorous irony that there were many fishermen
among Jesus' disciples. Interestingly, he also chose 12 disciples,
which, including himself, makes the perfect rugby league team.

"Rugby league has been the vehicle through which I have
lived my life. It's where I have realized much of my success,
experienced many of my failures, and met most of my friends.
Most importantly, it's where I came to Christ. I'm fortunate to
have had many opportunities to share my faith in Jesus and
profess that all things in his absence are – in the Ecclesiastical
sense – utterly meaningless.

"The first time I met Allen I was giving my testimony at St Peter's Church in Doncaster back in 2015. We chatted afterwards, having realized we had the great game of rugby league in common.

"We stayed in touch, and while following his work I heard about this intriguing biography, which tells the story of a man whose life reached a level of living hell that would have made Dante's imaginative blood curdle. In what seems like an impossible struggle, we are reminded in Allen's story that nothing is impossible with God.

"Allen's journey challenged me, encouraged me, and gave me a renewed zeal to live for Christ in my own walk with God. We often live in a structured, legalistic world, but Allen's story – as in scripture – reminds us that God uses those who are born-again in Christ in the most unfathomable and wonderful ways.

"John 3:8 says: 'The wind blows wherever it pleases. You hear its sound, but you cannot tell where it comes from or where it is going. So it is with everyone born of the Spirit.' And so it is with Allen Langham, it seems.

"God bless you."

Jamie Jones-Buchanan, professional rugby player for the Leeds Rhinos

TAMING OF A VILLAIN

A Message of Hope

Allen Langham

MONARCH

Published by
Lion Hudson Limited
Wilkinson House, Jordan Hill Business Park
Banbury Road, Oxford OX2 8DR, England
www.lionhudson.com
ISBN 9 7808 5721 937 4
e-ISBN 9 7808 5721 936 7
First edition 2019

Acknowledgments
Scripture quotations marked NIV taken from the Holy Bible, New
International Version Anglicized. Copyrwight © 1979, 1984, 2011 Biblica,
formerly International Bible Society. Used by permission of Hodder &
Stoughton Ltd, an Hachette UK company. All rights reserved. "NIV" is a
registered trademark of Biblica. UK trademark number 1448790.
A catalogue record for this book is available from the British Library
Cover image © allanswart/iStock
Printed and bound in the UK, February 2020, LH57

CONTENTS

FOREWORD

Cleddie Keith

The power is in the telling. I know Allen Langham. I have worshipped with him, broken bread with him, fellowshipped with him, corresponded with him, met his friends and people who believe in him. It was my privilege to meet his beautiful daughter, and watch him beam with pride as he introduced me to her and one of her friends whom she brought with her to a gospel meeting in Enfield, England. His is a story of hope to the dysfunctional and addicted world we all live in. This is a story of scandalous love and the relentless pursuit of God for those who feel there is no hope. This is the story of a cold case file being solved, of someone everyone thought so dead in sin there would never be a break in the case. Allen's story is the reason you "never put a never on a man", because God can raise that man up from the never-land of sin and its consequences, and use him for his glory. Hurt people hurt people, and this was Allen's story. He was a man with so much pain in his life the world tagged him "Bangham", and he became a beloved son of God.

– *Cleddie Keith*

Pastor Cleddie Keith and his wife Gaynell serve as the senior pastors of Heritage Fellowship in Florence, Kentucky.

Chapter 1

PINK WEDDING

The party was in full swing, music and dancing, and the bridegroom's smile was enormous as he shook my hand.

"You," he exclaimed, "are an inspiration!"

I thought, *really?*

I'd never met the guy before. I'd been invited by the bride, who was a member of PinkLadies, the health and fitness club that I ran from November 2014 to November 2018. Somehow I'd not thought to ask about her new family. Now I found out. The groom had invited a whole load of his friends from work, as you do.

They were all policemen. An official representative of law and order was telling me, Allen Langham – ex-offender, thief, criminal gangster, debt collector, drug addict – that I was an inspiration. Me, who used to have an "Approach with caution" tag on his police record.

I wondered if he knew who he was talking to. Of course he did; that was why he had said it.

There was a time that no police officer would have dreamt of shaking my hand, on duty or off. I'd been in rooms full of them before – but only after I'd led them a merry chase, usually resulting in violence and injury, meted out impartially by both parties. As much as women were objects of fleshly desires, officers were objects of authority, and I would go straight into attack mode.

I had spent most of my adult life in trouble with the police, or about to get into it, or on the run from them – that's when I wasn't locked up in jail. I was a violent man, and as soon as you put a pint in me, I was even more violent. I had absolutely no reason to love the police, nor they me.

But the Allen Langham who shook that man's hand had recently been voted as "most inspiring individual" at the Doncaster Community and Voluntary Services Awards. I also won a group award for the best community project.

How did, or could, this happen? Quite simply, Jesus Christ took a damaged, hurting man and transformed him miraculously. It blows my mind that people in authority could see me as an inspiration, but it's not me that inspires – it's what's in me, and that comes squarely from God.

My social media is littered with people who would never have had anything to do with me in my former life. Another officer messaged me a few months ago: "Hi Allen, you might not remember me but you assaulted me in the town centre. I just want to say how in awe I am of how you've turned your life around. There's no ill-feelings. Anything that happened between us, it's all water under the bridge."

And we're going to meet up for coffee.

In late 2018, another of the PinkLadies got in touch: "Hi Allen, I just want to say a huge thank you. I can't tell you how much boxing has helped us this year. We are now approaching the year anniversary on Thursday since we lost Dad, and you and the boxing have helped us through it. We've punched it out, and physically as well as mentally it's helped all of us, as well as prepare us for the wedding!"

It's not so great for everyone, of course. On another occasion, I bumped into a lady called Mary. You'll read about her in passing later on – she gets hit with a chair when I smash a bar up. She got caught in the crossfire – I wasn't aiming for her. At first I was just going to walk straight on in, but when I got as far as the doorway, I heard a voice inside, urging: "Just go and say hello." So I wandered over and asked how she was.

"Yeah, I'm fine," she answered, "considering how much you hurt me."

I could have just said, "Ah, that was a long time ago." Not to her, it wasn't. But the Bible says I am a new creation (2 Corinthians 5:17). The old has died. I can't change what happened, but I know God has forgiven it; I can only pray that for people like Mary, that truth will come to mean to them what it does to me.

Time and time again I've bumped into people from the past. Most have given me grace, though a lot of people still wonder, *Is it a scam? Something to get him out of prison?* I think I've shown I am consistently different. When the favour of the Lord is over us, it is transparent. To anyone who knows what I once was, the way I now live my life speaks volumes.

I got a message on Instagram from a guy who used to sell drugs for me. I'd absolutely battered him because I caught him with a woman I was seeing. He said, "Bro, you're really doing this. You know what, at first I had a laugh with all that religious shit, because you know where we're from it's all a myth. But with PinkLadies, charities and now this, hats off to you, proud bruv, bless up big things."

Just how I came to give my life to Jesus was an absolute miracle, but I will save that story till later.

Chapter 2

THE ALLEN STICK

I nearly didn't make it into the world at all. I was born in January 1978 during one of the coldest winters on record, with the snow piling up six feet deep. Friends have since joked that perhaps it was there to cool me down, knowing what a fiery tearaway I was to become. I spent the first several weeks in an incubator with yellow jaundice. My life was threatened, and it was touch and go for a while. But I pulled through and subsequently lived on a rough council estate at Copley Crescent, Scawsby, Doncaster, with my mum, dad, and sister Catherine. My parents were not married, which in itself led to much teasing and bullying as cohabitation wasn't considered the norm then as it is today.

I don't remember my dad ever being around, as I was only eighteen months old when he left home. He literally just stepped over me and walked out, so I'm told, having packed his bags. It was that abrupt and final. So I built up a lot of resentment, anger, and hatred towards him as I grew up. As a result my brother-in-law Pat, married to my eldest sister Rosemary, became my father-figure and role model, and I effectively had three mums, with Catherine also stepping into that role. I was thus the little favourite, often smothered in love. But that got confusing as it was mixed with much violence.

The general view was that I needed "toughening up" with what became known as the "Allen Stick", which was liberally wielded by my mum, who would lash out at me one moment and then smother me with affection the next. As a result I developed a pretty distorted, mixed-up view of what love really was as I became hyperactive and hard to control. When the "Allen Stick" was not available, there were other fairly lethal weapons at hand, including a high-heeled shoe and the spine of a roller-blind. On one occasion this was about to be swung around my backside after I had cut up a mattress with my penknife (I was traumatized when my dog Lassie, a Collie cross, had to be put to sleep and this was my reaction), but fortunately it missed and went clean through the wood-panelled door. Another time I was taken to hospital after falling into the fire during a tussle with Mum. But, as I was to understand much later, the violence I experienced from her was born from a life of much frustration and many hard knocks, not helped by my shocking behaviour.

My mum felt embarrassed because she was already in her forties when she had me – everyone thought she was my grandma. In fact, she'd always worried about what people thought, and had a rough time of it before I came along. Her first husband died after falling out of a truck while stationed in Germany with the army. She married again, this time to a Scottish painter, who throughout a twenty-year marriage beat her black and blue when he wasn't in prison. He used to drink with my dad, who subsequently hit it off with my mum and moved in. Then I came into the world and he upped and left. So all I ever knew in my early years was my mum and two sisters, and I flattered myself by reckoning I was the "man of the house".

My miserable young life very nearly came to an abrupt end when I was run over, aged just two. I had managed to escape through a side gate onto the main road, only to get knocked over outside our house, sustaining a head injury. Some folk later wondered if that might have contributed to the many crazy antics in which I subsequently became involved. I can't say, but the tragedy was that the driver responsible for my injury was later killed on the road himself after also being knocked over.

My mum did her best for us; she wanted to give me everything I needed and I remember thinking that I was going to take what I wanted out of life. She was a woman of integrity and high morals, and was keen to avoid getting into debt. She listened to Glen Miller and Elvis, but her mind was always somewhere else as she sat rocking in her chair. She suffered heavily from depression and used to eat a lot to compensate. Everything revolved around her. There was always noise and cigarettes –

my family smoked like chimneys. But much of those early years are a bit like those smoke-filled rooms – a fog, something I have subconsciously blanked out of my memory, including much of the violence.

I know I suffered abuse at the hands of a friend of the family, a black lady who used to bath me when I was somewhere between eight and ten years old. She would fondle me and force me to touch her. Unfortunately it made me feel very antagonistic towards black people and even as an adult I never went on a date with a black woman. It turned me into a racist, but all that was eventually to change in a very dramatic way. I'll tell you more about that later. There was a boy a few years older than me who used to live over the road, and his mum used to get us doing strip poker. And then we'd be having a sleepover and he'd start touching me. There was also abuse involving someone else, but I cannot recall the details except that it related to a man in a trilby hat. Even under hypnotherapy I could only remember going up the stairs with this man, blanking out as soon as I got to the bedroom. I just know there was some kind of abuse going on.

As a small boy I went to church on Sundays, getting all togged up in my suit. I went on my own, and even joined the choir and got confirmed. Fatherless and abused at home, I felt scared and I felt different. For some reason, I felt safe and at peace there. I spent a lot of time with other people's families, and at school I was very clingy with the teachers, attaching myself to them at every opportunity.

I just didn't want to be at home. Looking at photos of my early schooldays, I look like a little lost boy with such a sad face. But I loved football – in fact, anything to do with sport – and fishing. Everywhere I went, I took a ball with me. I was naturally left-footed, and because Pat taught me how to use my right foot I learnt how to play with both feet. As for fishing, I would head off to school, then bunk back and wait till my mum left. Once she'd gone, I'd reach through the letter box for the key, get my fishing gear, and head off to nearby Cusworth Hall to go fishing in the lake at the foot of the hill.

Although the estate was "working class", it was very much divided into two camps – those families whose men were actually working down the nearby coal mines and the many whose "breadwinner" was unemployed. In fact, there were two separate queues for school dinners, which reflected this social structure, the children from non-working homes being automatically stigmatized because their parents were on benefits which meant they didn't pay for their meals.

But I wasn't safe on my own outside. I was the youngest kid in the street, and because my dad was not around, and my parents hadn't been married, the older kids used to kick me around and call me a bastard. I was the little scruff who was easy-picking for the neighbourhood bullies, and I simply got battered on a regular basis. I always kept going back for more because I wanted to be accepted. I even got beaten up by a teenage girl. Admittedly she was a few years older than me. She would lie in wait for me behind some bush and pounce on me. It was all very humiliating.

My dog Lassie followed me absolutely everywhere, and we'd walk for miles. My safety was in the woods, where the dog and I would escape into the fantasy world of Mark Twain's *Huckleberry Finn*. I adopted Huck's character and cut off the bottom of my trousers, which also made my mum mad. It made sense as they were generally hand-me-downs from much taller boys, and I had short legs. But I would also be beaten by peers, who would wait for me in lonely alleys, or behind bushes, and lay into me with their fists.

Another character I took on was that of an army sergeant major, complete with camouflage outfit, shouting commands befitting my role as I tried to hide my inner pain. I just wanted all the kids on the street to like me. I was forever getting involved in scraps, but always came off worst. So I started to lash out at those a little younger than me, kicking them up and down the place as my peers did to me, passing on what I was receiving.

I joined the Cubs and later Scouts, and that became my escape. I loved those days going on camping trips, orienteering, marching around, playing five-a-side football – and being with people who wanted to father me. The Scouts were very much family to me, but the lure of fishing eventually pulled me away, along with a growing lack of discipline. The sad thing was that many of my positive male role models were from the Scouts. "Gone fishing" became a regular message I would post through the door for my mum.

Cusworth Hall, where I'd go to fish, was a short walk away. It sits in parkland at the top of a hill and has always been my secret place. Every major decision of my life, before and after my conversion, I've made there. I've held services there on the lawn, and it's where I started PinkLadies. As a kid, I would go there to play with my friends – we called ourselves the "Famous Five" – and fight with kids from the Balby estate the other side of the Hall grounds.

Sometimes I would sit at the top of the hill, taking in the astonishing panorama of Doncaster, and think, *One day I'll own you*, like some kind of gangster. Of course, that's exactly why the Hall was built there in the first place – the people there *did* own Doncaster. Nowadays, I can sit at the top of the hill, taking in the view, and be at peace.

But there wasn't a lot of peace back then, and it was about to take a turn for the even worse.

Chapter 3

MIGHTY BLOW

I was lying in bed late one morning, having got in late the night before, when I heard Rosemary come in downstairs. A moment later I heard her scream. I ran downstairs and found my mum lying dead on the settee. She had passed away in her sleep with what turned out to be a cerebral haemorrhage. I was just fourteen.

It was the morning after Bonfire Night, which I had spent with my rugby pals. What made matters worse was that I had fallen out with Mum over some minor issue when I came back in, and I hadn't put it right, or said a proper goodbye. It was a disagreement over money, and I remember her saying, "I hope all my debts are paid before I die." I had then demanded to know where my Weetabix was. She got upset and I stormed up to bed without kissing or cuddling her.

I put my hand on my mum's neck to see if I could feel her pulse, but it was the coldest feeling I've ever had in my life. She still had a cigarette in her hand, which had burnt a hole in her nightie. My sister was hysterical.

Then it was a blur. The house was full of people and I remember the next-door neighbour telling me, "Be a man! Dry those tears; there are women present." Someone wanted to know what medication she was on and I got out all her pills for inspection, trying to be responsible, trying to "be the man" as instructed. But Pat, my brother-in-law, showed more compassion and understanding. He took me by the hand and led me through to see her, taking off my mum's necklace and giving it to me.

My whole world fell apart. That was the point at which something changed in me as I felt this big ball of anger rise up in my stomach. I know I never really wanted to be at home because of the violence and chaos, but there was also a sense in which I knew I was safe. I found solace there for some reason. It was a launching pad for adventures into the woods, where I had dens and secret tunnels. But now it seemed like it was all being taken away, and I felt like kicking everything in my path. Up to now I had been the victim of bullies, but things were going to change from now on. Something inside me snapped, and the next time I got accosted by a bully, I vented my pent-up fury as I laid into him and battered him. I felt real release after that, but it was the beginning of a pattern of behaviour that was to land me in ever-deeper trouble as the fireball of anger starting rolling.

The upshot of all this was that I got expelled from a second school, Don Valley, not far away from Ridgewood Secondary School from which I had earlier been booted out over a catalogue of issues – messing about in class, fighting, selling my free dinner tickets, disrespect, truancy, repeated lateness, shoplifting, and, as my testosterone levels kicked in, coming on too strongly with the girls, like pulling their bra straps and that sort of thing. One of the mums complained that I had been suggestive towards her daughter.

I had just started at Don Valley when my mum died. But my reputation went before me, and I would swan about as a sort of Jack the Lad, which had the girls swooning over me. Part of the trouble was that I actually found the work too easy. Academically I was in the top sets for everything. But I needed to be the "class clown", showing off to the girls, scrapping and fighting to show how tough I was, and even sampling some "soft drugs". What kept me going for longer than would have been the case for other students misbehaving so badly was the quality of my work, and I suppose there was some allowance for me having lost my mum. There were even teachers who retired sick on account of me!

I moved into Catherine's home in nearby Sunnyfields. I always thought she and her husband Barry were cool, "with-it", and trendy, and somehow more lenient and lax with rules. But I soon realized there was tension between my sisters over the money they could claim for having me. So I would switch from one household to the other, which was very unsettling of course, though Rosemary and Pat were my official guardians, Rosemary taking on the role of my mum, whose death she has never fully got over.

With training hard for sport – more of that in chapter 5 – I was really into clean living, in the sense that I wouldn't smoke and I spent a lot of time working out in the gym. But I was something of a contradiction because I did begin using cannabis at this stage – and, yes, I do believe it's addictive. A group of us would form a so-called "bongbush", each chipping in about £2.50 in order to purchase a "healthy" stack of the weed. I have to say that, in the midst of all my turmoil and roller coaster of emotions, the short-term effects of the drug seemed beneficial, though of course they only masked the darker reality of my life at the time. I would go all giggly as I gradually sank into oblivion where nothing mattered as all my troubles were blocked out. Somehow this all fitted in fairly comfortably with my tough rugby training schedule, and I was able to function at a high level of fitness with the help of steroids.

So I left Don Valley without any GCSEs, aged nearly sixteen, because the staff couldn't cope with me any longer. I was showing great promise, getting an A* in Business Studies in the mock exams (for which I had given a presentation on Tupperware) and top marks in all the rest of my subjects except technology. The last straw was when I performed a "moonie" in front of the school governors! For the uninitiated, this is a form of insult achieved by showing off one's bare backside. The governors were busy touring the premises when I banged on the window and lowered my pants. Of course the class loved it, but neither the headmaster nor the governors were in the least bit amused. Looking back, I don't blame them.

My next stop was a school for "bad kids" in the town centre which I was able to attend only part-time in order to spend the rest of the week working on building sites. It seemed that I was going places, in one way or another. Perhaps life would take a new upward turn now that I would be mixing with adults and earning some money.

Chapter 4

PUNCH-DRUNK

My sister Catherine used to help run a pub called the Roman Ridge, which became something of a family concern as my mum had also been the cleaner there. Even before my mum died I used to spend a lot of time there, especially as I became seriously involved in rugby. Some of the older guys would take me under their wing and one of them was a notorious hard man who also loved Rugby League.

I joined in with the rest of the family at the Ridge where I would collect all the bottles and change the beer barrels. That took me into the cellar where I would help myself to lager. When mum was around I had been very anti-drink and drugs, but following my mum's passing, I threw that discipline out. From the age of about fifteen I had started to drink with my mates, and we were often to be found partying in the park. My outlet on the rugby field hadn't dulled the personal torment I felt inside, enforced by constant jibing about how worthless I was.

So alcohol helped to drain the pain. Unfortunately, it would generate anger at the same time, because the more I drank the more emotional and upset I would get. And that would often spark fights.

I was also mixing with the older guys at the pub and on the building sites where I began working while attending school part-time. They became my role models. So I got into the way of thinking that this is what a real man does, and it encouraged me all the more to drink, fight, and sleep around. I realized later that, as the Bible says, bad company corrupts good character. I built up a reputation as a good fighter, and it became something of a sport, which was initially restricted to our local area but then spread to other parts of town. It got to the stage where I was going around different places fighting for money in car parks and other such places. Yes, I was actually paid to beat people up, sometimes for the purpose of debt collection. I would come up against gangs known as Mods and Skindeep, and there would be running battles between groups from Scawsby and nearby Balby. This led to a terrible tragedy when my friend Carl Tracey died after being stabbed, but it didn't stop the mayhem. People would wonder how I could be so good at fighting, because I wasn't that big or strong at this stage. But when love turns to hate it's a powerful force. I had got stamped on so much as I grew up that a boy reaching out for love had been turned into a monster. Everything revolved around the pub, and we were always down there cooking up some scam or wheeler-dealing some dodgy business arrangements.

There was a particular group of men who took me under their wing. Billy was one of them, and we used to arm-wrestle with each other. They used to gamble, play cards, and they would send me to the bar or the shop to get stuff for them. It made me feel welcomed and wanted. Shane used to ruffle my hair and give me £20, or I would knock on his door at 6.30 p.m. on a Friday and he would give me cash. We would walk down to the York Bar Working Men's Club and work our way up to the Roman Ridge, and then the Sun Inn. On Friday nights there was a disco at the Ridge, where there was a clear division between the smoke-filled tap room with cannabis and ecstasy flying around, and the lounge where the older generation would congregate. Respect for the older generation had been instilled into me and I would address them as "Mr" and "Mrs".

It seemed that everyone in those days took me under their wing. There was all kinds of skulduggery going on; there was a "Del Boy" wise guy character who grew up opposite us. He would carry around a "wedge" of money (a tightly packed heap of notes) and drink a lot. He was easy come, easy go, and would throw his money about, but there was always some scam on the go.

Everything revolved around that pub and I would go there every day. I would move from one job to another, but all I really wanted to do was go to the pub. My best friend at the time was Clifford, and when trouble broke out I felt I needed to prove myself to these guys – that I was tough and could handle myself – because I wanted them to look up to me. So I ended up street fighting, giving back some of the grief I was getting at home by taking out my anger and frustration on whoever stood in my way. I started pumping iron and getting stronger until I had a really devastating punch. Just as I was the little lad who fetched and carried for my elders, I would soon have some of my peers running about for me and began to build myself a little "firm" – a group of young people who happened to collide together in their collective emotional turmoil. All of us had issues and we would get drunk, take drugs together, "pull" the girls, and fight. We were effectively a family, which is something I always craved, having lost both my father and mother. But I always felt unfulfilled because, though I was the hard man externally, I was probably the weakest of all inside. So I did whatever it took to get accepted while others would manipulate the soft-hearted kindness within me that was the real me. Yet I was seen as the "fixer" of my peers' problems, fighting their battles, so to speak, because they admired my macho behaviour, and I played up to that.

One day a chap called Tom had been celebrating all day on the back of a big insurance payout, and was very disrespectful of the women in the bar when he came sauntering in. My sister was in charge at the time, as she often was, and he was getting "mouthy" with her. Little did he realize he had picked the wrong fight, because I was particularly protective of Catherine and was at the same time standing up for the other women, encouraging them to sit with me and come under my protection.

I was frustrated that I felt unable to provide the protection my sister needed, so the next time it happened, things turned nasty. The upshot was that I was told there was a guy called Jim wanting to meet me outside. I took off and, as soon as I walked through the door, I saw him out of the corner of my eye lunging in to attack me. I turned around and whacked him repeatedly, beating him up good and proper. Flushed with success, I subsequently invited Tom outside and gave him a hammering too. It was a big scalp in the area. I think my sister was very proud of me, probably revelling in the fact that her baby brother had come to her rescue so dramatically. From then on my confidence surged and violence became as much a part of my life as sleeping, eating, drinking, and drugs. That's also when I realized I got a sexual turn-on from violence, which seemed to attract certain women because I would usually end up taking one of them home after winning a scrap. After all, I had fought for her reputation and was getting paid in kind! It was a sweet taste of victory over fear of people like Tom.

All the while I was also trying to fit rugby in – training with a view to a career in the game – which meant I was living in two worlds.

Chapter 5

HAVING A BALL

It wasn't always rugby. I originally wanted to be a footballer, with the lofty ambition of playing for England. From the day I watched TV coverage of Argentina winning the World Cup in 1986 (famous for the "hand of God" incident through which Maradona scored a controversial goal) – I was just eight at the time – I worked it out in my little head that by 1994 I was going to be the first-ever sixteen-year-old playing in the World Cup. And it was through my involvement in the Cubs and Scouts that I was given much encouragement. The local bobby, PC Berry, charged with doing what he could to keep kids off the street, took us under his wing and would meet us on the Rosedale Primary and Middle School playing field. That's when I grasped the whole idea of teamwork and sport. I duly played for the school team in five-a-side competitions, and we never got beaten. The seven of us (including two subs) then formed the nucleus of the eleven-a-side team as we got older, and I also played in a local Sunday League side. Our coach was an ex-professional called Derek Cross who had a dodgy knee and strictly adhered to a defensive form of the game played by the Germans with his best four players at the back. It was all very disciplined and organized. I was pretty speedy and on the ball with one-touch tactics, and I always wanted to play in midfield, but was stuck in defence. I did have an exceptionally long throw-in and could get up and down the pitch in no time, being very fit from walking and rambling in the woods along with bike riding, sometimes all the way to Bridlington and back (125 miles). But I was a bit naughty at school, and, when I missed a game through detention, I remember sitting forlornly in the classroom crying my eyes out.

I was proficient at all sports, though in basketball I could never get the ball into the hoop. At least in that respect I was "having a ball". By the time I was twelve I was playing Sunday League with the Adwick Owls U13s. By now I was at my first secondary school, Ridgewood, where my form teacher (who was also a Scout leader) followed the Doncaster Dons professional Rugby League team. So I started playing rugby too. We were the only school in the whole of South Yorkshire with a Rugby League team. Our only regular opponents were Minsthorpe High School, just across the border into West Yorkshire.

As soon as I picked up a rugby ball the whole dynamic of my life changed. It was clear that I was naturally suited to the game. In fact I had virtually been playing rugby on the football pitch with being so boisterous at tackling. I didn't realize until much later that my father (who of course I didn't know as a kid) had actually played for the Dons. So one day I went down to their training ground with a friend who played for their junior side and, on seeing that I was naturally gifted, they took me on. I was just twelve, and the youth section was based on the playing fields at Toll Bar on the northern outskirts of the town. So now I was playing rugby on Saturday and football on Sunday, and I was also in the school athletics squad for the 200m and 1,500m.

Perhaps conscious of my speed, I was put on the wing for my very first game of rugby. As soon as I touched the ball, I scored a try in the corner – only to be told off because the idea was to get it as close to the central posts as possible to make a conversion kick simpler. Obviously I'd had time enough to do that, but I didn't really understand the game yet. I repeated the offence, scoring in the corner, at which point I was moved to the middle from where I doubled my tally, finishing up with four tries on my debut for Doncaster Boys.

I scored several tries each game as we won the Yorkshire League that season, and I was named players' player of the year, settling down at prop forward, usually in the No. 10 position. I loved the camaraderie, travelling to matches in a rickety old minibus, and later in a battered Nissan Micra that used to shake when we topped 60mph.

There were times when I was really happy. I suppose, looking back, rugby has been the one consistent thread in my life.

There was a lot of competition for getting trials with Doncaster Rovers, as most boys had only footballing aspirations, and I too had trials with them, along with Rotherham and Yorkshire Schools, but didn't make it in the end. I was a very good footballer, scoring fourteen goals from defence as captain of the Owls that season when I also became squat-thrust champion (a training exercise).

But I was clearly an exceptional rugby player; it was time to choose between the two. The choice was made easier by my falling out with the Owls coach, who was also my Scout group leader.

My second rugby season was much tougher, as I was in among older boys and it coincided with my mum's death. At the same time I was getting a taste for alcohol, and would get accustomed to performing at a decent level under the influence, emerging with flying colours even with a chronic hangover on one occasion. Yet it was around this time that my rugby really took off. I was training with the professionals by my mid-teens – even with the first team – and at sixteen signed a YTS (Youth Training Scheme) contract with the club, for which I was paid £50 a week. That meant I accompanied older teammates, including overseas players like South African Jamie Bloem, into various schools where we took part in coaching sessions with the boys. It was ironic – even bizarre – that I even returned to Ridgewood, not as a student but effectively as a sports "teacher". I enjoyed coaching in schools with some of the star players, and even had pupils asking for my autograph. In fact I became quite handy with my signature. Things were looking up. Jamie, by the way, ended up in trouble for taking performance-enhancing drugs in the form of steroids.

Meanwhile Doncaster got promoted, and to comply with the rules governing Division 1 clubs an Academy side was formed known as the Kingfishers. As well as competing in a league, we would play in curtain-raisers for big games, and I well remember the electrifying atmosphere when we hosted Widnes in the Challenge Cup. On this occasion we played after the main match so we didn't have to worry about making a mess of an already muddy pitch. The senior team had been beaten squarely 40–10 when we took to the field. I duly scored three tries and was top tackler and man of the match as we hammered our illustrious opponents, putting some fifty points past them.

It all helped to restore my personal esteem, as I was often made to feel worthless in other respects, particularly at home. Now, on the pitch, I was out to prove I was somebody. There was a time when I was playing both rugby codes (League and Union), but I realized I needed to concentrate on just one of them. Dave Wandless was our coach, and most of the players were from the Wakefield area, some 20 miles north.

By sixteen I had left school and was supplementing my earnings from rugby with a job working for an electrical firm. I was also regularly mentioned in dispatches in the sports pages of the local newspaper as we progressed in Division 3 of the Academy League. It was my best-ever season. In a match against Rochdale Hornets, I sparked a fightback on seventy-three minutes when I "struck with a good solo effort from 20 yards, leaving would-be tacklers flat on the ground". The report said I had been "turning in some outstanding performances" and I scored again as we trounced Huddersfield 48–10. I was man of the match on several occasions, including the time we triumphed 62–22 at Hunslet. That report described me as "a local lad who has been patient in waiting for his chance to prove himself, scoring quick tries with hard driving and excellent work in defence". And I once more led a fightback against Rochdale, this time setting up victory over an undefeated side with a perfect record until then. The report described how "the robust figure of Allen Langham came thundering onto a short pass from Martin Brown and scooted round the posts".

Despite all the many unhelpful distractions of my early life I made great progress in the sport, and at seventeen I signed for Sheffield Eagles, then in the Super League, which is the RL equivalent of football's Premiership. I really wanted to play for the Dons, but they had gone into liquidation at that point, and, although there had been talk of a merger with Sheffield, just 25 miles away, it came to nothing. (The Dons did later rise from the ashes.) Oldham and Hull Kingston Rovers had also shown interest in me. Oldham offered me a five-year contract and Hull a two-year deal, but I opted for a three-year contract with Eagles worth £3,000, as Sheffield was on the doorstep and the money was a lot for a teenager from a poor background. What's more, I had good people investing their time in me and giving me work, thanks to the rugby connections. In fact, I had a job offer in Dubai.

I remember driving to the Sheffield ground in my newly purchased Ford Orion – bought with money left by my mum – with my best friend Rob, and showing him my fat cheque – a massive amount for a seventeen-year-old. Had I stayed on the straight and narrow, the next contract could have been for a substantial figure.

The future seemed rosy. I was living my dream, playing for a top club. After scoring four tries in a game for their Academy side (basically U19s), I was moved to the Alliance (second) team and played most of the season with them while also having a spell on the bench for the first team.

But I was already on a thorny path which wasn't going to be easy to get off. I had got into trouble with the police at just fourteen over shoplifting, for which I received a caution. Now I was playing rugby for a big club, but I was really living two lives because, at the same time, I was out on the town clubbing virtually every night, which was certainly not conducive to professional sport. And that's when my life started to unravel.

Chapter 6

A TICKING TIME BOMB

It had become apparent that I had a particular talent for fighting. There were soon some black eyes around, along with a bust nose, so the troublemakers started buying me drinks and sucking up to me. Billy, who had taken me under his wing and loved arm-wrestling, had a big influence on me, and, because I admired him so, I started to copy how he walked, and even wore the same kind of shoes. In fact, I also tried to imitate the characters of gangster movies like *The Godfather* as well as the infamous Kray brothers. I became obsessed with the Krays and would strut around like them with a mean expression on my face, looking for trouble. I had learnt that a real man was a fighting, gambling womanizer. For the first time in my life, instead of feeling weak, I felt powerful. Rage burned inside me because I had been hurt, so I would resort to intimidation and loved to see people cowering away from me in fear. I would create an argument just so I could unleash violence on the victim.

Afterwards I always felt so guilty, though I made sure I didn't show it. There was such a conflict going on inside me. I wanted to be loved, but at the same time it was like we were all acting out a gangster movie in our local pub. Yet I still felt lost and alone. Even though I was surrounded by lots of people, I always felt there was something missing in my life.

All my friends had problems. We found solace in each other, and by this time I had moved into my own rented accommodation, which everyone used as a dumping ground. I seemed to have no concern for where I was heading; I simply blamed everybody else in the world for my problems. I loved my close circle, but I was very unpredictable, always feeling let down and rejected. My life was absolute chaos. I never knew what was going to happen next, and I had a fear of ploughing ahead because things always seemed to go wrong.

My reputation was spreading and went up a further notch when I managed to floor two members of a well-known boxing family. Billy put his arms around me, saying, "You done good!" News spread about how I was fighting Billy's battles. We were surrounded by women who, though apparently attracted to violent men, thought they could subsequently change them and turn them into domestic pussycats.

We were out five nights a week, and then we would start going down to the town centre a couple of miles away – downing pints, "snakebites" (beer mixed with cider), and double-shots. I used to walk up the High Street boasting to my mates, "Watch this for a left hook", and there would be innocent folk laid out on the pavement – all simply in aid of showing off to the lads. We would then start raving and partying at nightclubs, and it was at this time that I started getting arrested. I would be charged with fighting in the town centre and held in police cells overnight. I was just seventeen and had a criminal record, accumulating quite a few charges in a short period.

I signed for Sheffield Eagles in the middle of all this. It was a Premier League rugby club for which I needed to be fit and strong, and yet I was drinking and taking drugs. Fortunately I was naturally gifted, which masked things for a while. I was more bothered about getting a pat on my back from my peers than applying myself to the hard graft and discipline that a future in rugby demanded. We didn't believe in rules or regulations, or even the law itself. We were a "firm", fighting and selling drugs like ecstasy, which we started bringing back to the village. As a result, some of the older generation began getting "off their heads". After training I would have up to fifty people partying at my house, which was turned into a cannabis-smoking den. Because I was feeling rough all the time through these round-the-clock parties, I was also on amphetamines to pick me up for rugby.

And because I was getting stronger, the scraps were getting more violent. I was very unpredictable, flipping into a rage at the slightest provocation. I was obsessed with being the hard man, showboating in front of an adoring public. For the first time in my life I felt I was somebody, which I craved so much. The irony was that, in the cold light of day which I rarely experienced at this time, I already was something of a minor celebrity, having signed for a top professional rugby club. But somehow that didn't seem to count for much in my own back yard where I basked in this "nice" feeling of being able to cause others to quake in fear.

About this time Cliff had come into my world. He was "top dog" among a group of older boys, with a flash car, money, and nice clothes. Although white, he wore dreadlocks and was into rap and hip-hop. And he had the most evil, piercing eyes, which forced me to turn away. Just the look of him would frighten us all, but he was the only person to whom I could fully relate. We built a relationship based on mutual respect. His dad was a successful businessman, and Cliff was working for him. And although he moved in the same circles of skulduggery as we did, he was a grafter, working hard at painting and decorating. He got me involved in martial arts and started taking me to ju-jitsu classes, which meant I was now training at a different level – I had also taken up boxing – all of which served to instil some discipline into my street fighting as I learnt about chokes, pressure points, and the like. I excelled in these areas and built up a raw strength which, mixed with drugs and alcohol, amounted to a volatile cocktail.

Cliff and I became a force to be reckoned with. He felt sorry for me, and I manipulated that side of him as we indulged in drug-fuelled parties at my house, which became the place of retreat after the clubs closed. Eventually we were raided by the police, and I was arrested and cautioned because it was my property.

Strangely, however, I remember feeling quite content that summer of 1995. We would go jet-skiing at a place called the Blue Lagoon some miles north of the town, and I was working for Doncaster Rewind, refurbishing industrial motors. I had treated myself to my first car – the Ford Orion, with a pull-out stereo. I also benefited from my Sheffield Eagles contract and had more money than sense. My training regime was only part-time – two days a week – and my income needed to be supplemented by other work, but I kept changing jobs as I struggled with the discipline involved – especially on cold, dark nights – and life started to take a dip.

From the age of twelve my big ambition had been to be a professional Rugby League player. Now I had achieved that, I wasn't content and it was no longer my primary focus. Yet I was excelling on the pitch. I suppose there was an element of complacency in my attitude, thinking I could keep up this façade of top-performing sportsman while at the same time mixing with criminals and indulging in a culture of drugs and nightclubs. The latter was merely a mask for how I was feeling. I was seventeen stone of pure beef! In my mind's eye I was never going to be hunted again, so I had turned myself into a mountain of muscle. But it was all in response to fear. I was usually the one who started the trouble and, even if I hadn't, I generally finished it off. It seemed that trouble followed me wherever I went.

The writing was on the wall. I was in self-destruct mode, a ticking time bomb waiting to go off. My mum had died on Bonfire Night, and as the anniversary of her passing came around every year, it seemed to trigger me off into trouble. I was still in that mode on Christmas Day when I got involved in a brawl outside the Mallard pub after another bout of drinking with my friend Robert, whom I referred to as "Reg" (after Reg Kray). He used to call his mother "Ma" in the same way as the Kray twins apparently talked. His dad had left for another woman, after which Robert had gone off the rails. Anyway, that night he and I took on a father and son. I chased the son, he the dad, and they both got badly battered. Yet I felt no remorse. I remember how we laughed about it, and went partying the next day as if nothing had happened. But the victims had reported us to the police; we were arrested on Boxing Day for a double assault, for which we had to appear in court where we were given community service and a probation order. It would prove to be the trigger of an eighteen-year cycle of crime and violence. Now I was in the "system". I was given 240 hours of community service and a year's probation.

I didn't learn my lesson and failed to turn up for the community service, and as a result things were much worse when I got mixed up with the next fracas. Yet I had reason to get myself sorted as I had started my first serious relationship with Anna. I always wanted to be married and have a family, so we got engaged. In the meantime I lost my job at the Rewind factory over time-keeping issues and my rugby was deteriorating, despite having broken through the Academy into the second team and even being a substitute for the 1st XIII. I was about to throw it all away.

Anna went out with another lad, and when he dropped her off, I went into a jealous rage, jumped into my car, and chased him through the streets. His escape route was eventually blocked at a level crossing where the gates had come down, so I shuddered to a halt, grabbed my crook-lock (for locking the steering wheel), rushed over to his car, and starting banging on the window with what amounted to a lethal weapon. I managed to smash through the glass and badly injure the man, who must have wondered what was going on with this crazy guy chasing and shouting and now hammering him over the head. Of course, he didn't know who I was, so I thought I'd got away with it.

Anna then told me she had left her house keys in the man's car and asked me to retrieve them. Suddenly I was very frightened; I wasn't as tough as I made out. Nor was I very clever, as I was obviously going to give the game away in the process. The man was hospitalized with a head injury for which I was charged with serious assault, and then given bail pending trial. I admitted what I had done, but disputed the version of events given by the victim, making out that I was acting in self-defence.

While on bail, instead of keeping my head down, I carried on causing trouble regardless, responding to provocation in a nightclub by grabbing the bloke's tie and headbutting him, busting his nose. Robert then put his hand up a girl's skirt, which provoked her boyfriend into a rage. So I knocked him over and duly followed Rob, who was being dragged downstairs by the bouncer. In trying to elude arrest I was sent flying over the bonnet of a police car. Nothing came of it all at that point, and I was released next day.

So we were back in town the following evening, clubbing again, when Rob "pulled" a girl and asked for the keys of my car so he could have his way with her. But unfortunately it wasn't as straightforward as that. He decided to help himself to some nice-looking wheel trims in the car park while he was about it, and then I too managed to "pull" a girl and set off to reclaim my car. The end result was that all of us were arrested on suspicion of theft and piled into a riot van. Rob was going ballistic, presumably over the indignity of it all, which prompted a police officer to shut him up by knocking him out with his elbow. I just saw red and lashed out at a succession of officers, at which point the driver slammed on the brakes and the doors flew open, with another officer getting kicked as he jumped out.

I was arrested for assaulting four policemen, while at the same time I was facing an aggravated bodily harm charge for the injury I had inflicted on the man at the level crossing, another over the headbutting incident, and had also failed to complete the community service hours to which I had been sentenced earlier. Clearly, I was in serious trouble as my life collapsed around me like a house of cards.

When my case finally came up I knew – and everyone else did – that I was facing a prison sentence. My first. I had used up every last chance and it was with nervous apprehension that I entered the court following an emotional breakfast with my sister Catherine. The big, brave man – six feet and seventeen stone – was fading every minute, and I now felt just five feet high and three stone. I thanked my solicitor for his help, but I knew in my heart that it had been to no avail, and it didn't take long for the magistrates to come to a decision. I knew what it was before anything was said as the Group 4 security people had made an appearance. I was sentenced to eight months in a Young Offenders' Institution – six for actual bodily harm and two for breaching the probation order. Eagles promptly cancelled my contract for bringing the club into disrepute.

It was April 1996. I was just eighteen and was about to start a fifteen-year revolving door in and out of prison for various offences, mostly to do with uncontrolled aggression. I walked into Doncaster's Marsh Gate prison, in the same town centre where I had caused much of the trouble that landed me there, feeling alone and isolated, with no purpose or sense of direction and no positive role model. At that point I gave up all hope.

Chapter 7

HEROIN HELL

Although I was fully expecting it, my anxiety really started to kick in once the sentence was announced. I was taken downstairs in handcuffs to a holding cell with up to a dozen others. I was wearing a suit, so I stood out like a sore thumb. The others seemed rough and ready, laughing and joking as they lit up fags and inserted drugs into their backsides. This was known as "plugging", something with which I was to become familiar. I couldn't believe how they were openly getting people to stand around them while they carried out this manoeuvre undetected. I wondered what I had come to. I felt like a small, scared boy again, helpless and lonely, far away from the man who had beaten up four police officers and committed a series of other violent offences, trying to work out how long it would be before I was released from this nightmare. I knew in theory that with good behaviour it would be four months – half the actual sentence, which is usually the case. But four months is a long time for a teenager, especially when locked up and without knowing exactly what prison life has in store. We spent the first two hours in this holding cell, and were then re-handcuffed and marched out to a bus. It was at that point that the reality began to sink in.

At first, you'd think we were going to a football match. It was a rowdy scene with people shouting and bawling. But as the engine fired up, an eerie silence descended on the prisoners. Then the radio came on, playing "Wonderwall" by Oasis, and tears filled my eyes as I remembered the last time I had heard that song in a pub full of life and laughter. I thought of what I had left behind, of the rugby career I had thrown away, of my sisters who cooked all my meals and cleaned my house, and my nieces and nephews who idolized me. I also thought of the fights, which flashed through my mind in slow motion as the five-minute drive to Marsh Gate felt like hours.

I had never been in a prison before. I kept telling myself not to show any weakness or emotion, and to be strong. But inside my heart was breaking. I was taken into the induction wing and the first thing that hit me was the noise. Then everyone stared at me and it all went quiet.

"What you in for? Have you got owt? Got any burn?"

Immediately I was being pestered for drugs and cigarettes, and within minutes I had no baccy left. And with me looking oh so smart with my suit on, everybody was taking the mick.

"What are you, a solicitor or something?"

I was so naïve, and had brought only one change of clothes, which meant that my visitors would have to top me up later. I put on all this bravado, making out I was Jack the Lad and tough as old boots. But as soon as my cell door closed behind me, I flopped onto the bed, sobbing. Teatime came and I found the quietest table as I realized the rest of the inmates were sussing me out. I wasn't small, of course, so that alerted a few people on the wing. Many of them mistook me for a gypsy with my wavy blond hair, as they were notorious for trouble and fighting. I discovered there was a rivalry between South and West Yorkshire inmates, so the Sheffield, Barnsley, Rotherham, and Doncaster lads would take sides against those from Leeds, Bradford, and Halifax.

When I returned from tea my room had been turned over, with most of my stuff taken. All I knew about prison had been gleaned from watching television's *Cell Block H*, so I looked for the Bea Smith character who was the de facto top dog on the wing, duly reporting the theft and demanding it back. The dog in question nodded his head, walked off, and subsequently gave me back my top, but nothing else. I asked who had taken it, but didn't get anywhere. I stood my ground, but inside I was shaking like a leaf. These guys were streetwise; I was naïve. I did everything on impulse. Strictly speaking, I was not criminally minded. I had to go to prison to become a criminal.

Prison life was all about routine. We were woken up at 7.15, and this was followed by breakfast, exercise, bang-up (roll call three times a day), education/work, the gym, and the TV room. I was used to violence, but not without the Dutch courage fuelled by drink, which brought out the rage in me. Yes, I was capable of looking after myself, but I wasn't streetwise. I was totally out of my depth and couldn't relate to these people. I was a big softie, a loving guy at heart whose mates questioned my sexuality as a result, though I slept with enough girls to allay their fears. Some of them were definitely uncomfortable with my "touchy-feely" persona. You see, I had this burning desire to feel accepted, and the only time I fully felt that was when I came into a relationship with Jesus. But I'm running ahead of myself.

So I started wanting to get accepted by guys from whom I should have stayed well away. I built friendships with these prisoners, which included burglars and TWOCers (Taking vehicles Without the Owner's Consent) from Manor Top, a rough part of Sheffield. And they were all taking heroin! I didn't realize what it was, even though I had seen it at a rave, but my cellmate got hold of it from a visitor. The currency of heroin in prison was probably ten times its street value. I had already taken ecstasy, amphetamines, and cannabis, and thought this was just another drug. So I started smoking it with my cellmate. Soon I was floating in a sort of heavenly glow of complete euphoria, blanking out all fear, anxiety, and pain. Years later I would discover it was effectively a counterfeit of the experience of being filled with the Holy Spirit. Instead of building you up in a godly way it actually destroys you. Instead of taking you on a trip to heaven, it leads down a destructive path to hell.

Before long, a fortnight had passed. In fact, the next few months were simply a blur. I was receiving letters every day along with visits from family and work. I got a job on the wing as a cleaner and started training with the gym staff, slotting in with them beautifully as I lifted some serious weights. I also served food, which is very useful currency behind bars.

The atmosphere in prison could change dramatically from one day to another. Some days would be happy, accompanied by rave and rap music, while other times could be quite depressing – and a high self-harm and suicide rate reflected that. There was a punchbag on the wing, presumably to help inmates vent their frustrations rather than just train for the boxing ring.

Quite a few incidents occurred while I was there. Once there was a hostage situation, in which the kitchen was barricaded over some protest. It was a red-hot summer, and inmates would sometimes refuse to come in from the yard after exercise. The prison was run by the prisoners in those days (it had only opened in 1994). The staff had no control. I was on the South Yorkshire wing, and we used to torture the West Yorkshire men, especially the Asians, with electrical shocks. There were just two members of staff on a wing of up to seventy inmates, and no cameras!

Drugs were rife and it was a massive culture shock to me. But instead of keeping my distance, as I should have done, I wanted to be involved as I searched for acceptance. With the tobacco and food to which I had easy access, I had plenty of currency for a supply of heroin. And with being able to lift nearly 200 kilos, I was outperforming the gym staff – after all, I had trained with New Zealand rugby internationals – so I was well in with the "big lads".

I started peddling drugs as well as taking them, having learnt from fellow inmates that it wasn't just a case of needing money to pay for drugs – I could actually make money out of it. It was so easy to get hold of them through visitors. Despite earlier promises to my family that I'd never let it happen again, I went from Mr Nice Guy to being more aggressive and intimidating. The young "firm" of friends out to cause general mischief in Scawsby were now all starting to do a bit of "stir" (jail) as they tried to ape the menacing world of some of the more notorious gangsters in their distribution of drugs for illicit cash.

All in all, it was a four-month fast-track education in criminal behaviour during which I learnt how to steal a car and carry out various scams, including credit card fraud. The irony was that I was let out for "good behaviour" after serving just half my sentence.

When I was released, I had lost all contact with the rugby club. I had no job and nowhere to go. All the waifs and strays used to come to my house, which became a drug den. So, from being a professional rugby player, within just a few months I had become a heroin and crack addict as I pressed the self-destruct button.

I was actually still on bail for an offence committed before I started my sentence, and now awaited trial for this one. I had been charged with homophobic affray in an incident that took place as I walked home from town with three friends. A car ran over the foot of one of my friends, whose mate then kicked the side of the vehicle. The guys inside jumped out and hit the perpetrator, but we subsequently battered the pair along with two more who came to their assistance. A tooth came through the lip of one of them, and I had to stick my hand in the snow to stop the bleeding from the blow I had landed with my fist.

Ten minutes later the police caught up with us, and, with ripped shirts and blood pouring from my hand, we were obviously not innocent. We were initially arrested on a charge of violent disorder, which carries a substantial prison sentence, but nobody could really determine who had done what. I had learnt the "no comment" routine from prison, but I was named in a statement, and because they had been drinking in a notorious gay bar the homophobic tag was employed, along with grievous bodily harm and other offences. Fortunately the solicitor found a loophole, managing to insist that all the evidence was heard by magistrates before it could be committed to Crown Court, knowing full well that there were witnesses who did not want to come to court for fear of lewd behaviour being revealed (one of them was married). So a deal was struck tying everything up in "affray".

We were looking at up to two years in jail, but in fact five of us were given six months apiece, and I was deemed the ringleader. I was buzzing over the shorter than expected sentence because by then I was madly in love with my first real sweetheart, Bonnie. As it happened, I served the usual half-sentence, twelve weeks, nine of them in an open prison at nearby Hatfield which amounted to the life of Riley in some ways. But it was also the longest twelve weeks of my life – absolute torture – in view of being smitten by young love. My thoughts were constantly on what Bonnie was up to. Anyway, no longer naïve following my first stint at Marsh Gate, I was well prepared this time. I came in with some cannabis "plugged" to give me some "currency", and a big bag of clothes, along with cigarettes, other drugs, and loads of paper! I now knew everybody and slotted into the role of trying to be one of the top dogs on the wing.

Clearly aware of my form, lads from Bradford and Barnsley were giving me heroin within two days to get me on their side. Rob and I were together to start with, but once at rural Hatfield, I fell on my feet thanks to having a driving licence and was given the cushy job of tractor driver on a farm run by the prison which enabled it to be self-sufficient. Actually, it was a like a boot camp because we had to run everywhere, and on Fridays we did cross-country. Since I was reasonably fit that was no problem, and by this time I was back in training with the aim of returning to rugby on release.

Despite my anguish over missing Bonnie, I loved it on the farm, although we were cruel to the pigs. If they needed antibiotics, we'd give them an overdose just for the kicks. We would strike the pigs on the head with a bar and they would lie on the floor, quivering – we said that the pigs were raving. When I'd done my bit of cleaning out the pig swill, with the help of the tractor, I would lie in the sun by the river. The job was all over in an hour. But my heart was booming with love for Bonnie and I didn't want to see or speak to anybody else. I wrote love letters every day, and got myself clean and fit.

When I came out we decided to move in together (well, she moved in to my place, which meant I had to kick out my friends). I resolved to get my life straight and decided I was going to set up a sports coaching business. Things were looking rosier all round. I was working for her dad on a building site, though I was still drinking and heavily involved in the distribution of cannabis. We would go out partying and were enjoying life as a newly established couple. I had a car, a house, a beautiful blonde girlfriend. What more could I want? But the "honeymoon" didn't last long.

All was fine and dandy until one day I found myself playing with a one-arm bandit slot machine, having dropped Bonnie off at the hairdressing salon where she worked. And who should I bump into but my old cellmate from Marsh Gate – the one who got me on heroin. He said he was "rattling" (having painful withdrawal symptoms) and needed a fix of the lethal drug. In a moment of madness, I decided to help him find some, and I was soon hooked again myself, still naïve as to its power. In no time I was spending the money I was making on cannabis on heroin. I didn't realize at that stage what it was doing to me. Over the next six months I was living two lives – life at home with my girlfriend, and life in the murky world of drug-dealing. My daughter Emily was conceived, but it would be three years before I was able to have any contact with her. I was running out of money with using heroin every day, which also made it increasingly difficult to work properly, and I was now gaining the reputation of being a smackhead. When my source dried up, the next thing I knew I had developed flu-like symptoms. I thought I just needed a rest, but my friend told me it was a sign that I was hooked – I was now an addict.

Sure enough, after smoking a wrap, the symptoms left me. Suddenly I couldn't stop myself and now Bonnie was pregnant. A huge surge of fear swept over me as it dawned on me that I couldn't even look after myself – my sister was still cooking for me – never mind being a dad. To add to my problems, I was getting behind on my cannabis payments. In no time at all I had neither cannabis nor heroin because I had no money, and I was trying to keep everybody from knowing about my dilemma.

To make matters worse, my ex-cellmate and heroin buddie moved in, which quite understandably didn't exactly please Bonnie, who told me to get rid of him. Meantime I was trying to confess my situation to her, but she just laughed it off. When it became impossible to keep my addiction a secret, she went hysterical and left the house.

Around this time I was locked up for a week on remand over an incident at a christening party, which ended with a drunken free-for-all in someone's back garden. Once again I assaulted a policeman and then tried to bite him, but once more the solicitor found a loophole, which was that it turned out none of the officers who arrived on the scene had read me my rights. To be fair, they were probably too busy defending themselves from attack. It came to trial, where I was charged with actual bodily harm on the police officer (I had shattered his cheekbone) but, because no one had cautioned me, I got off. I would say that this was the only time when, firstly, I really deserved prison and, secondly, I needed it! On those earlier occasions I was more in need of mentoring and help, and now I needed to get off heroin.

Another downside of this outcome was that, in an apparent attempt at revenge on their part, I seemed to be getting arrested virtually every day as the cops turned up the heat on me. Bonnie and I got back together for Christmas 1997. But I stupidly sneaked off to buy some heroin and two hours later I was out of my face and couldn't eat any dinner. It all came to a head and she left me for good, after which I spiralled out of control very quickly, taking drastic measures to feed my habit. I was selling furniture (which wasn't mine to sell as the house was rented) along with my car and a gold chain (which I did own). And when I needed £600 to pay off a cannabis debt, I took down the radiators and boiler system, for which I got arrested later. I then moved into a flat with a friend called Charles, for some reason painted his bedroom luminous blue and green, sold his microwave, and even burgled my brother-in-law before selling on the stolen items in the village. It was low-life behaviour at its worst and even my friends ganged up on me, telling me they were "kicking me out of the village", which was a serious threat as they had a mafia-type control of the area and crossing the line was not an option.

I subsequently moved into the town centre, dossing down wherever I could find temporary residence – even in the Red Light district – and shoplifting on a daily basis to pay for drugs, racking up loads of theft and dishonesty offences over a short period. It was hardly surprising that my family didn't know how to handle the whole messy business – my sisters were absolutely distraught, though Catherine began studying for a social work degree to try to understand it all. I was no longer the presentable young lad for which I had gained a reputation. I looked a mess, I was stinking in clothes I wore for weeks at a time, and then there was the smell of heroin. I couldn't even go to the toilet properly due to the effects of the drug on my digestive system. I had gone from the hardest man in the village, being paid to collect debts and beat people up, to a down-and-out in the town centre knocking around with prostitutes and the homeless. Daily life was focused on stealing, living off chocolate bars and milkshakes, trying to get the next £10 for another fix.

Days drifted into weeks and months. But at last some light appeared on the horizon. I was on remand for theft. My probation officer, with the help of my sisters, tried to get me a place in a rehabilitation centre in Sheffield as an alternative to a further prison sentence. I was duly accepted, funding was sorted, and I was expecting to be sent there when I next appeared in court. I was banking all my hopes on this – my life, my future, my family, my new daughter. All this was at stake. But Judge Bennett wasn't having any of it. He argued that because I had been on probation before and had failed to comply with my order, he had no alternative to passing a custodial sentence of three months, which meant I had just three weeks left to serve, and I knew I wouldn't be able to get off heroin in that time. So I lost hope; I totally gave up.

I was indeed released three weeks later. I was still detoxing, as expected, and craving a fix. I was handed a £30 discharge grant, but I reckoned I needed more than that, so I stood outside waiting for a guy who I noticed had come off the sex offenders' wing. This made him fair game; sex offenders are regarded among prisoners as pariahs who deserve special punishment. I saw him sign the ledger for £385, which he had presumably left for safekeeping on entering the prison, so I plotted an attack together with a fellow inmate who was released with me. I launched into him with my fists and my accomplice took the money out of his pocket. We split the cash and went our separate ways. I spent the windfall with someone I met inside who lived in Stainforth, a few miles out of town, and it all went up in smoke within just two days. So now I was homeless, back on heroin, and just happened to bump into a guy I knew who was a burglar. I had a heroin debt to settle, and I needed a fix, so I agreed to be a lookout for a burglary – for a fee, of course.

In the space of just one week, I had robbed a sex offender, run up a drug debt, and been an accomplice to a burglary. My fingerprints would eventually give me away. Meantime I went on a shoplifting spree around some of the northern suburbs before setting out on a long walk back to town. It was then that I was sure I heard an internal voice saying, "If you don't sort yourself out, you're going to get locked up." Having dabbled in the world of spirit mediums – which I now know is strictly forbidden by God – I thought it was my mum at the time. But maybe it was God himself. Despite this warning, I called in at the big Morrison's supermarket on the edge of the town centre, grabbed two bottles of whisky, and walked out, only to be followed by a security officer. Thinking on my feet, I simply turned round and walked straight back in. But I hadn't fooled anyone and was still arrested for attempted theft. I was also charged for the street robbery outside the prison (the victim had gone straight back inside to report the incident) and remanded in custody. I was looking at a two-and-a-half year sentence, but the magistrates somehow let me out on bail the following week.

I reckoned things couldn't get worse, but I was wrong.

Chapter 8

KIDNAPPED, AND NEARLY KILLED!

I have described how I only just survived my initial hours in this world, and then how I was almost killed as a toddler when knocked down by a car a couple of years later. And now, as the day approached for the birth of my first child, I was very nearly taken off the scene once again. The combined negative effects of being pushed out by Bonnie, along with the prospect of not seeing my baby born (I was told I'd be arrested if I attended the birth), being kicked out of my village, and my family not speaking to me all served to further fuel my drug addiction. In fact, when in July 1998 I heard Emily had been born, we celebrated with a crack and heroin party. At least my sister Rosemary was with Bonnie for the birth.

My life would hang in the balance during a terrifying kidnap saga – all the result of over-stretching myself and getting too greedy. For the first time I had started to loiter with heavy-duty heroin dealers. They hung out in Balby, on the west side of the town centre, and were linked with a notorious group based in Bawtry, a village to the south of town. One of them, Frank Cook, was a trigger-happy gangster, often armed with a shotgun, who made a name for himself by shooting up pubs in a manner akin to movie scenes about the Wild West. These were literally the big guns of the drug scene, and it was how I got introduced to crack cocaine. One of the gang, nicknamed Brownie, took a liking to me and I became his driver and runner.

The first time I took crack I sweated so profusely I had to take my shirt off as my heart was pumping like crazy, and I ended up running around thinking I was a chicken! But I got a taste for it, even though it gave me the shakes. We would find ourselves doing hair-raising and very dangerous things – such as, when driving at over 100mph on the way to Sheffield, Brownie would take over the wheel from the passenger seat. When we got there – somehow in one piece – we would mix with Jamaican gangsters who were about as dangerous as the reckless driving we had just experienced. We would hide any jewellery, phones or other valuables as they would rob or defraud you given half the chance. It was like entering the lions' den of the drug world. On one occasion after we'd "scored" (made a successful purchase) a stash of crack, we kept stopping for a smoke on the way back and, when the effects had finally worn off, Brownie took a large amount of temazepam (used for treating insomnia), which turned him into a monster as he proceeded to smash up our digs and fall out with his friends.

So I took him to a "safe house" – the flat of a single mum where our hoard of heroin was hidden. But when he fell asleep, an evil thought came to my mind, encouraged by my growing addiction, which meant that any loyalty I felt towards him went out of the window in a flash. I also had access to the car and so, in one mad moment, I decided to steal the heroin, leave the area, and make a fresh start on the east coast. I figured that with that quantity of the drug I could both feed my habit and set up a new life for myself. I was just planning my escape when I bumped into some friends – a guy and his girl – who decided to come with me, only they needed to go back to their place to pick up some of their belongings. Trouble was, it was just around the corner from where I had left a sleeping Brownie. But I didn't think clearly or sensibly when I was high on drugs, although the girl agreed to keep the heroin hoard in her knickers for safekeeping!

I was just driving over a bridge when I saw a car coming towards us with some of the big guns inside. They immediately spun around and gave chase and, in panic, I turned left, only to find it was a dead-end street! They all jumped out with baseball bats, and as I covered my face in defence, I urged the girl to run off. They battered both me and her boyfriend and then took us back to the safe house, where I was now a kidnap victim suffering extreme violence. They soon let the boyfriend go, but continued to rain down blows on me, repeatedly smashing my hands with a hammer. I told them I had panicked when I saw them, thinking they were after me for some other reason, but that I had no idea who had taken the heroin.

A succession of other suspects – anyone who had access to the house – were also brought in for questioning and duly stabbed, battered, and even stripped naked in the process of trying to establish the truth. But they all knew that I was responsible. I was eventually allowed to clean myself up and get something from a nearby shop. They had the whole area covered by their spies, so they knew I couldn't escape. It was really a trap to see where it would take me, and it worked, as I legged it straight to the home of the girl hiding the heroin on her person. But there was no one there, and I had been followed. All the guys piled in through the back door, duly trashed the place, and, putting a knife to my throat, dragged me outside before bundling me into the back of their car. They made some phone calls and told me I was being taken to Frank's and would not come back alive. A knife was now being pointed at me from both directions as I sat in the middle; it was probably the scariest situation I've ever been in. I had seen what they'd done to people they knew to be innocent, or at least ignorant, of whatever it was they were accused of. These guys would smash people's hands just to get information out of them. So what were they going to do with me? I thought I was a dead man.

When we stopped at some traffic lights, I grabbed a now-or-never opportunity, headbutting the guy to my right with such force that both of us fell through the door. I got up and ran, but was knocked over the head with a bottle and then over the back with a baseball bat before colliding head first with a lamp post. Fortunately we were near the train station, and the Transport Police came running out to help. I was lying in a pool of blood and they took me into their office. I knew my life was in jeopardy, but getting the police involved would only complicate matters further with all that I was up to. So I headed for Scawsby, despite being barred from the area, and found temporary accommodation in the empty house of friends who had just moved out. There was nothing left except a bath and I proceeded to strip the place of copper.

However, the noise I was making alerted neighbours, who duly called the police, and I was taken into custody for my own safety, as they'd heard on the street grapevine that I was going to be killed. As usual, I did not cooperate with them and I was released without charge the following day. But the heavy gang were on my tail, so I hatched an escape plan. I returned to Scawsby once more, stole a Nintendo computer game, and sold it for £100, which paid for a stash of heroin and a coach ticket to London.

I had nowhere to run; I was extremely fearful and anxious, not knowing what to do. Everything I needed was gone – my sisters, my child, my respect. So I decided to run away from it all and lose myself among the bright lights.

It is only by the grace of God that I am alive today.

Chapter 9

HOMELESS IN LONDON

I boarded a coach bound for Victoria Station in the heart of the capital, panicking that the police might be on my tail and getting paranoid about it. I started to plan how I would begin a new life in London. I would start by finding some close friends of mine there. I would literally reinvent myself by using an alias – the name of a friend who had not crossed swords with the police. But as a chronic heroin addict I was making a bit of a spectacle of myself, acting totally out of character, sweating profusely and making silly noises and generally waffling away with phrases that seemed to make perfect sense to me. What's more, I was becoming over-friendly. These are classic symptoms of being high on drugs, which gave me a false sense of security. Halfway into the journey I was warned to calm down or I would be kicked off the bus.

It was late at night when we finally arrived. My first impressions of London were of the sheer size and scale of it, along with the frantic busyness, with thousands cramming the pavements, coming and going despite the hour. Fear crept over me as I realized that this big, tough character I was supposed to be was really very vulnerable. The fact of how far I had fallen dawned on me. I felt so lonely, and was missing my family, still with deep feelings for Bonnie. Worried and anxious, I shed tears wondering what I was going to do. My friends lived in Hammersmith, a few Underground stations along the line. But it was getting late and I soon discovered how, in London, a new world comes out at night, with increasingly shadier characters appearing on the scene. People were trying to hustle me, and, although I had wised up somewhat in prison, I still had much to learn on the matter of steering clear of unwanted attention. I discovered the streets of London were not paved with gold – in fact, they were lined with beggars and dropouts. I had no money – just a bag of drugs in my pocket – and I remember feeling real fear.

My friends were no longer at the address I had, so now I was really stuck. The only other person I knew in all of London was a dancer working at Stringfellows, a nightclub in the West End featuring a bevy of scantily clad, leggy ladies. It was a very long walk, several miles, and it was 2 a.m. when I eventually arrived there and joined a queue on a big red carpet outside. A doorman shoved me aside as if I was a piece of rubbish and I was sent flying onto the pavement. The indignity of it all left me feeling so unworthy and scruffy, which I guess was how I looked – weak and totally out of my depth. I started to panic and called the club on my phone, pretending to be my friend's brother James who needed to speak to his sister about a family emergency. But they weren't having any of it; no one was allowed to interrupt their employees' work schedule.

I took the tube to Brixton, a notoriously rough neighbourhood south of the Thames, and as I came up from the Underground there were these black guys all lined up outside, blatantly asking, "White or brown?" This was dealers' slang for crack and heroin. It's virtually a no-go zone at that time of night, so there was no police presence. Anyway, I opted for one of each, and then asked to borrow a pipe. The next thing I was getting chased, and I instinctively grabbed a stick and waved it about in a bid to scare them off. As I continued to tramp the streets, the drugs were wearing off and I was growing extremely weary.

Then suddenly I saw this place like a church with a light on and knocked on the door. A nun answered and took pity on me, offering a place to sleep for the night. Looking back, I suppose that was a real divine encounter, which meant that my first night in London was spent in God's house. I guess that was where God started to stir in my life. But all I felt was pain, misery, and loneliness in a place I didn't know. As low as I had sunk, I didn't think it right to smoke drugs in such a place and I had a beautiful, peaceful sleep. Of course, I didn't want to leave when I woke up, but I had no option. "You have to go now," the nun insisted.

I spent the last of my money on a cocktail of crack and heroin which wiped me out to such an extent I can hardly recall the rest of what happened that day. The drugs in London were a lot stronger than I was used to, and they knocked me for six, leaving me slurring my words and experiencing everything in slow motion. I ended up in Leicester Square in the heart of the West End, but I don't know how I got there. I was so tired, and my feet were aching, and in my panic over how I was going to get hold of drugs I resorted to shoplifting. Body Shop gift sets are pretty easy to conceal as well as simple to sell on. I just found the nearest pub and sold them within minutes of stealing them.

This kind of "trade" was such a money-spinner that it took me to a new level of drug use. I would end up on my feet for twenty-four hours a day unless I could find a night shelter offered by one of the various organizations reaching out to the homeless. And – I suppose inevitably – I soon found myself in Soho, just a few blocks from Leicester Square. I hadn't realized just how depraved and seedy this area really was. I was petrified. Organized crime was all part and parcel of the scene, and at a dangerous level I had never experienced before, with guns and machetes being flashed about liberally as Chinese Triads and London mobsters fought each other in ongoing battles for territory and business. Some of the wealthier Chinese living there were dangerous gangsters. They would kidnap their own, torture them on film, and then send the recording back to their families, demanding money. I also saw people being tortured for their money by ruthless gangsters from Albania.

I managed to find a street dealer there who became a good source of top-quality gear, though I did get ripped off once or twice. I began to congregate with others who were doing the same thing as me; many of them had also set out for the bright lights with visions of streets paved with gold, just as I had.

I began to knock around with a bloke called Wolf; in fact, I collected quite a few hangers-on thanks to my shoplifting expertise and even started taking orders from working girls, which was safer because there was a big risk of being arrested with trading in pubs. The prostitutes would buzz you in. Some of them had pimps ostensibly watching out for them but in reality making a mint out of their sexual activities. Some were virtually enslaved, forced to perform depraved acts including acting out scenes in a torture chamber. Many were also highly addicted to crack and heroin. I was terrified, and I knew that I was getting a little too close to the point where I wouldn't be able to pull myself out of this degrading lifestyle; however, it was to be a major turning point, as I will describe later. The girls would give me a list of items they wanted. Sometimes they paid me up front, and I started to get drugs from them too.

Sleeping arrangements were very hit-and-miss. I had to face up to the fact that I was homeless and destitute. If I couldn't get a place in a hostel, I had to camp down in the street with everyone else in the same predicament.

There was a nice shelter for the homeless in Soho where they would provide plenty of food along with a shower and a bed for the night. Staying there on the odd occasion was like Christmas had come, especially with all there was to eat. I would normally restrict spending on food to the bare minimum in order to have as much as possible to satisfy my drug habit.

At the same time, shoplifting was becoming too risky as I started to get recognized in the stores, so I resorted to pestering tourists for money – simply begging, really. I had to invest in a suit (well, actually I stole suits worth up to £1,000), as it made sense to look smart and presentable. Then I would come up with some sob story for poor unsuspecting foreigners that I was just £2 short, or perhaps up to £8, of what I needed to get home. And they invariably fell for it. I managed to persuade one American couple that, if only I had £60, I could have a bed for two days. Well, they took me to McDonald's, bought me a meal, got me a work interview with the manager there for the next day, and handed me £100 in cash. The wife wanted to take me back to America and adopt me! Needless to say, I never turned up for the interview and didn't see that sweet couple again. I just hope they'd forgive me if they found out what I was really up to.

Once I had a smart suit on, it was easy to steal another. I'd walk into a shop, choose a new one, and go into the changing room, where it would become my undergarment, then cover it with the clothes I came in wearing before walking out as if butter wouldn't melt in my mouth, actually wearing two suits in one! The more blatant I was, the more likely it was I'd get away with it. The key was being smart and cool. On one occasion a security guard unknowingly helped me steal a suit. If you were blasé and confident enough, acting like you weren't doing anything wrong, you could get them to hold things for you and open the door. You could defuse their suspicion by asking them for help. I also specialized in stealing shirts and ties – I would wrap as many as twenty ties around my arm and simply walk out and have them sold on in no time.

A funny episode was when I stole some equipment from a sex shop – a rather large rubber replica of a male organ – and ended up being chased around the streets carrying it. I managed to lose the police in Chinatown but the prostitute to whom I hoped to sell it wasn't interested. So that proved a lost cause for no reward.

Now a chronic drug user spending up to £500 a day on crack, I traded in deception as I manipulated others including friends, fellow addicts, and prostitutes. My way of life descended into a pit where everything was dark, dangerous, deceitful, and deadly. I guess I was manifesting what the Bible calls the "works of darkness" as I continually sowed seeds designed to satisfy "the flesh" – the cravings of sinful man. I knew nothing of "sowing to the Spirit" which the Bible says reaps eternal life.

Amid all the seedy backstreets, there was a classy lingerie shop which, on closer inspection, was nothing more than a posh strip joint. Unsuspecting customers would be lured in by champagne and the glitzy decor, and offered the chance of having underwear of their choice modelled by one of the young female assistants. This might go on for a while as the customer succumbed to further modelling offers for a variety of lingerie. But now he was caught in a trap, because in the store's eyes he had purchased every piece of underwear modelled, and he would not be able to leave until he had paid for the lot – including the champagne! Some of them would end up getting severely beaten and, by chance, I once came across a man in a suit on a torture rack. They couldn't go to the police because they were usually wealthy businessmen who shouldn't have been where they were and who, during the lingerie show, would have been filmed in a compromising situation alongside topless girls. I realize now that I was effectively contributing to this man's torture by dealing with these people.

All this time I was living under the name "Carl Denby", one of my best mates from schooldays and one of the "Famous Five". Taking on another's identity proved confusing at times, especially when someone shouted my name and I failed to respond. The game was soon up, however, and I eventually got caught – not once, but twice. I got away with a caution on each occasion, but was kept overnight in the cells and sent to court the third time.

Living on The Strand was an eye-opener. The heart of London's theatre land, it was an environment with a bit of a "Jekyll and Hyde" personality, you could say – a select, very wealthy thoroughfare by day, and a rough-and-ready bed for the homeless at night, with the Salvation Army, Red Cross, St John's Ambulance service, and other charities all waiting to help with sandwiches and hot drinks, and giving out blankets and thick socks. The latter was much appreciated as my feet were now rotting from malnutrition. Sometimes I had all my worldly goods (which wasn't much) stolen overnight by fellow street-dwellers, so I learnt to huddle together in a group for protection. Then, early in the morning at around 6.30 a.m., I would have a nasty wake-up call as council workers came and hosed us down, just as though they were washing away the vermin to turn the neighbourhood back into the clean, scrubbed-up area for which it had a reputation. It was all very undignified and lots of abuse was hurled in both directions.

Before learning about safety in numbers with substitute families, I would sometimes find myself sleeping in a doorway on my own, but that brought unwanted attention, with homosexuals preying on me. On two occasions I was approached by men who seemed at first to be Good Samaritans. They offered me food, shelter, and a bed for the night. I'd get cleaned up and sorted out and was just drifting off to sleep when once I found this guy masturbating beside me. It was horrible. I felt a rage surging up inside me and could have killed him. But I was no longer the tough rugby-playing fighter;

as an addict I was weak. I simply gave him a lot of verbal abuse, grabbed a bundle of money, and left. The next time I was approached in this way, the man managed to persuade me that he had a heart for the homeless and a bottle of methadone (a heroin substitute) with which to stabilize me. But after taking a warm shower and the medicine, I naturally felt very groggy, at which point he too started making sexual advances towards me, groping and touching me inappropriately. This time I used more force and hit him with a speaker before running off and leaving all my belongings behind. He was conscious, but it was a very dodgy moment, a frightening experience that I found extremely difficult to handle. I thought people were being friendly, and ended up getting sexually abused.

Now I had no money and nowhere to go. So I started grafting again – working the shops for easy spoils. I would steal handbags, only for my Chinese bosses to wipe people's accounts out as they delved into the contents and hacked into credit cards. But since this attracted a lot of heat from the police, I spread out to new territory via an all-day Tube ticket, travelling up and down the Northern Line which took me to suburbs that were yet to have the unfortunate experience of being fleeced by me. More seediness and depravity followed and, flushed with success, I returned to the West End where I raided an Oxford Street store, picking up everything on my order list except one item. Then the long arm of the law finally caught up with me and rested on my shoulder. I was sentenced (as Carl Denby) to twenty-eight days at Feltham, a Young Offenders' Institution, and rang home, making out I had a job at McDonald's.

I was released after fourteen days, but they seemed like an eternity as I was in and out of tremors and I was giving meals away in exchange for tobacco. I came out with no belongings and just over £100 (given by the prison as a combination of a discharge allowance and having no fixed abode), and was chronically addicted to crack and heroin. I went straight back to Leicester Square to buy drugs, and, because I hadn't used them during my period inside, they pretty much knocked me out.

My card was marked now. I was in a mess and panicking. There seemed no way out, so obviously I was highly vulnerable. One day in Soho, a seemingly respectable, well-dressed man approached me offering a financial incentive, which I was free to negotiate, to go home with him. This was to prove a massive turning point in my life. If I had gone with him, I would probably have become a rent boy. He took me to this car park and I got into his upmarket vehicle. He opened his wallet, pulled out a stack of £50 notes, and peeled one off, folding it and placing it on the dashboard.

"That's yours, whatever you decide," he announced. "But what do you want from life? I'm a very powerful man; I can open doors for you."

My instinct was screaming, "Get out!" I knew there was

something sinister about it, and there would be no going back from this. So I grabbed the £50 note, jumped out of the car, and ran off, returning to my "safer" life of shoplifting for drugs as soon as I had spent the latest windfall.

Then, quite suddenly, I was stopped and searched by an undercover plain-clothes officer. I had nothing on me, but the police had made the connection between Carl Denby and the wanted Allen Langham. I was hauled off to the police station and was soon in a Group 4 security van on my way back to Doncaster. Bizarrely, when I appeared in court, it was for non-payment of fines, which I duly promised to pay. So it was merely a slap on the wrist and away you go. I even managed to fleece some drug money from my solicitor; I reckoned he could claim it back on legal aid.

I was hoping I'd got away with it and subsequently made an attempt at reconciliation with my family. I stole a baby outfit to present as a gift (and peace offering) for my new daughter Emily and duly turned up at my ex-girlfriend's place, but was refused access. So I went to my sister Rosemary's, where she and the rest of my family made me look in the mirror. I must have looked a dismal sight with a trainer on one foot and a shoe on the other, and out of my face on heroin.

"What do you think of your uncle now?" she asked her kids, who had held me on a lofty pedestal until then.

"He's a waster!" they chorused, at which point I blamed everything on my family and stormed off, looking to be taken in by friends. But they also turned me away. I had sunk to my lowest point, with neither friends nor family wanting to know me. So I decided – in a fit of desperation, I suppose – to return to London.

I had learnt in prison how to "black-box" a car by breaking the steering lock, and, though it took me all of twenty minutes, I managed to steal a Ford Orion from a pub car park. It was clearly a company vehicle as it was emblazoned with the firm's name, but that didn't put me off. I was soon speeding down the A1 towards London. I was doing 90mph near Grantham, some fifty miles south, when a tyre burst and I pulled onto the hard shoulder. But there was no monkey wrench with which to change the wheel, so I flagged down another driver and got it sorted. I was just about to drive off when I saw flashing blue lights in my rear-view mirror.

I quickly made up a false name and address, but the officers soon discovered there was no such house number for the road I had chosen at random. I was arrested on suspicion of theft of a motor vehicle and taken to Grantham Police Station before being transferred to Doncaster, where the next morning I was rearrested for the street robbery of the sex offender, being a lookout for a burglary, and the car theft. I knew I was going to be off the streets for some years. It was December 1998 and I was remanded in custody pending sentence. Although things were looking bleak and I felt such a failure at the time, I had at least walked away from becoming a rent boy.

It was just one of the many times I genuinely believe the hand of God was on my life.

Chapter 10

PRISON PAIN

The policeman who arrested me in Doncaster was DC Langham. He was apparently no relation, but it seemed strangely appropriate that my namesake should determine my destiny. He was quite relaxed and took me out for a cigarette – they don't do that now – and tried to see if there were any other offences he could add into the bargain. I was duly charged, fingerprinted, and had my DNA confirmed. I didn't really have much defence other than that all my offences were rooted in heroin. Once processed, I was put in a holding cell ready for a court appearance next day. Apart from supplying blankets and boil-in-the-bag or microwave food, these police cells were very spartan, noisy, and smelly. But prisoners couldn't smoke inside the station, even then, though sometimes coppers would use tobacco as an encouragement during interrogation. Just surviving the police station was tough, but I had managed to get a doctor to prescribe some sleeping tablets. I was charged with robbery, burglary, theft of a vehicle, and failing to appear in court, so I knew there was no point in even trying to make an application for bail.

Expecting five to seven years, my hard-man demeanour crumbled as the cell door shut behind me. I was absolutely distraught, and didn't sleep a wink that night as I reflected on my downward spiral over the previous couple of years. Although detoxing heavily from drugs and tobacco, I had a sense of peace because I felt I could now finally get myself sorted out. I knew I couldn't make it on the street without getting clean. But there was a raging battle going on within me. I so wanted to get back all I had lost, including my daughter, by getting clean… but at the same time I was desperately looking for the next fix. Now I was trapped in the cycle of addiction, not having the mental strength to fight the drug and yet wanting to do my utmost to get clean.

I was remanded in custody pending committal to Crown Court. It was early December, and on the short ride to Marsh Gate prison I had this sinking feeling that I might not see daylight for up to four years, as the severity of my situation hit home like a hammer. The detoxing was kicking in badly – I was shaking all over – as I was processed through reception. At this stage I either had to pull myself together, determined to stay strong, or crumble. I would need a hard skin and a lot of resilience to take what fellow inmates were about to throw at me. On previous visits, I had robbed everyone I could, beat people up, and pinched stuff, the thought of which left me in a state of chronic paranoia, wondering who I was going to bump into next. For example, the burglary for which I acted as a lookout was of an elderly man's house. Inmates are very good at establishing degrees of criminal behaviour, and picking on old folk was generally regarded as out of order.

All I had were the clothes I was wearing; I didn't have a penny to my name, had no support, and was heavily addicted to heroin and cocaine. I was at rock bottom, totally desperate. What's more, the prison was full, so I was put on the protection wing reserved for sex offenders, which meant the food would be contaminated – it would be spat on and worse by inmates in the kitchen who regard such criminals as the lowest of the low. Those of us who were not sex offenders would keep ourselves busy plotting to get at them in some way or other using an extraordinary inter-cellular telephone system which worked via the toilet pan. Using the toilet brush as a pump would have the effect of temporarily emptying the pan of water, creating an ideal vehicle for carrying sound.

Meanwhile, I was going through my "rattle" of coming off heroin without any medical help such as methadone substitute, which they have to provide nowadays to conform to European human rights laws. I was suffering from chronic diarrhoea, was burning up and sweating profusely with a severe temperature, yet felt freezing cold; I'd had no sleep and was headbutting the wall and biting my arms, which just seemed a better pain than what I was experiencing. I had some horrific hallucinations. It was as if I was in hell, engulfed in spiritual darkness with a horrible sensation all around me. I couldn't eat (well, it was contaminated anyway) and lashed out at one of the sex offenders with a weapon fashioned out of plastic cutlery, razor blades, and a toothbrush; it's amazing how lethal a weapon an inmate could construct despite all attempts to keep them out of harm's way. I was nicknamed "Bangham" because of my aggressive tendencies.

I waited three days before there was space on the Induction Wing. I was still officially a Young Offender, although my twenty-first birthday was now just weeks away. Until then I had merely done "baby sentences"; now I was facing my first long sentence. I kept wondering how I was going to survive it, especially as in those days a prisoner would have to complete two-thirds of any sentence of more than four years. So I was looking at the prospect of not seeing daylight until I was twenty-four and my baby daughter was five years old.

Although desperate to get clean, I was also desperate for drugs and, in a mad moment, I tried to sell my designer top for a bag of the hard stuff. But I got barely a sniff of it as I was fobbed off with a bit of powder residue which didn't even touch the sides of my "rattle". And now I'd lost £80 worth of clothing, leaving me with just a T-shirt on top. How long was I going to prolong the agony? For the next twenty-one days of detoxing, I had no sleep and crammed my stomach with carbohydrates and leftover puddings, but brought up most of what I ate. I was starving, yet at the same time developing a big belly from all the stodge. Christmas dinner went straight through me so that, as with the previous year, the festive season was completely lost on me.

Finally, after several weeks, I had my first decent night's sleep and woke up like a new man. I took myself off to the gym and my sister dropped off a bag of clothes. But it was very hard being locked up over New Year. It's a time when prisoners become particularly paranoid – over what their wives and girlfriends are getting up to, for instance. In many cases they live in fear of phone calls, visits, and "Dear John" letters, the latter typifying the ending of a relationship. It was enough to make a big, hard man crumble. If someone had just received bad news, the whole mood of the prison changed and turned hostile, with extra staff suddenly appearing on the scene.

Inmates are stripped of all their power inside a prison. We were sharing digs with some of the meanest men on the planet, but the most they could aspire to behind bars was being a tobacco baron or loan shark. The way that worked was that if a prisoner borrowed one razor, he owed him two! Phone cards and tobacco were the currency among inmates. Some even brewed hooch, using yeast, fruit, and sugar from the kitchen, which tasted disgusting, but it was like rocket fuel. It was unbelievable what we could make in prison.

When I went to the gym for the first time – complete with big belly – a guy called Sooty, who was in for armed robbery, punched me in the kidneys trying to intimidate me. It took the wind out of me, but when the men at my dinner table started ribbing me for it, I decided to take matters into my own hands. So I put down my tray, marched over to Sooty, and promptly knocked him out. I did the same to a friend of his who came to his assistance, and then another – until I discovered he was a prison officer. I was just about to kick his head in when I realized who he was. I was duly dragged off and "nicked" (charged), and had fourteen days added to my sentence, along with the same time confined to my cell and with loss of privileges. I was moved to another wing, and was taken by surprise when an officer walked in and gave me a hug – presumably I had done them a favour by tackling the bully boys. As a reward I was made the staff tea boy for the wing.

Being on remand, meanwhile, I was going backwards and forwards to court. And for my twenty-first birthday present on 12 January, I was moved to the "Cons" (adult convicts) Wing. I had been mixing with "plastic gangsters", as they were called. Now I was with the big boys. There was Concrete Ken, who had buried his wife's head in concrete, and a gangster from Leeds who had married into the Mafia and was in for armed robbery of a jeweller's shop. Doncaster had Category A status then, which meant it was built to house the worst criminals. No longer was my accommodation something akin to a decent bedsit; it was just a bare cell.

The wing rep, Dave Downs, was on remand for some very serious charges and had a fearsome reputation. Anyway, Dave took a liking to me, probably because of my rugby endeavours, and I started to train at the gym with him. By now I was getting physically stronger with regular training at the gym amid ambitions of playing rugby again. He also taught me to box and, through my association with him, I was adopted onto the top table of inmates best not to mess with. Surrounded by all these top dogs, I lived like a king, had all the best food, got into really good shape, and signed up for virtually every educational course going, gaining a series of qualifications in the process. In fact, we spent fourteen hours a day outside the cell.

But I foolishly took heroin again. A new guy came in with a parcel plugged up his insides, and I failed to resist the temptation. I also subsequently failed to avoid suspicion, and was duly kicked off the drug-free wing which had promised so much for me. I was heartbroken, as were my mates, especially Dave, who had encouraged me so much about having a right mental attitude. I was his protégé. Nevertheless, I guess the determination he instilled in me did eventually pay dividends.

Now I was banged up in "Beirut", an adjacent wing rife with drugs which acted as a dumping ground for serious criminals, one of whom had driven around Sheffield with a severed head in his boot. I started to deteriorate as I began dabbling with drugs again, postponing my good intentions of reformation until later, while I went through the motions of prison routine which involved building strong relationships with people, especially my cellmates. A Rastafarian would conceal spliffs in his dreadlocks, and a man from Stoke was supplying me with heroin. When he got nicked for failing a drug test, I agreed to take the rap for supplying him in exchange for a further supply. Then, when two brothers were caught thieving from other cells, the prison officers asked me to deal with them. I did what I was asked, but subsequently got accused of slashing the face of a sex offender, for which I was sentenced to a 23-hour-per-day lock-up in the segregation unit. It seemed that every time I started using heroin, my life and circumstances took a downward spiral. The message was gradually getting through, but it would take a while longer for me to change my ways.

Legendary Bible teacher Derek Prince has said that the closest a person can get to demonic possession is in either a mental institution or a prison. So when someone is in segregation, like a prison within a prison, they are under some severe oppression. Their only visitors are the chaplain and the landing officers that let them out for three meals and one hour of exercise a day. So they have the opportunity for maybe four brushes with other people. In the morning the officers take out the mattress, so the inmate just sits in a metal-framed chair.

I kept fit by doing press-ups and sit-ups, and I read the Bible every day to pass the time. It was the only book available and, although I also used some of the Rizla-like pages to make roll-ups (a fact that now disgusts me), I was genuinely imbibing some truth into my head as well.

Finally, in June 1999, after six long months, the day came for sentencing at Sheffield Crown Court. I was given three years, ten months and forty-six days, the latter being a separate count. That made it just two weeks short of four years, the threshold for turning it into a much longer stretch. I would now only serve half my sentence, although I was regularly racking up extra time thanks to my bad behaviour. But I was ecstatic nonetheless to have escaped much harsher punishment.

On the downside, my story was splashed across the front page of Sheffield's *Star* newspaper under the banner headline "EAGLES ACE IN HEROIN SHAME". Roy Emery's report ensured that everyone knew how the mighty had fallen:

Sheffield Eagles prospect Allen Langham's sporting dreams ended in misery today as he faced up to almost four years behind bars.

The promising prop's life has been torn apart by the curse of heroin – and changed a likeable sportsman into a compulsive thief.

At the age of 17, Langham, who started his Rugby League career with the Doncaster Academy, was destined to become a star at Don Valley Stadium after joining the Eagles. But the evil addiction took its grip on the teenager.

Sheffield Crown Court heard how Langham started down the slippery slope by going shoplifting to pay for his addiction. He ended up getting a short spell behind bars in Doncaster's Marsh Gate Prison.

But only yards from the prison gates he committed another spate of offences including punching another released inmate while an accomplice robbed him of £351 cash.

Before Langham was caught he paid off a £200 heroin debt by keeping watch on a pensioner's house in Doncaster while a pal burgled it.

Months earlier the 21-year-old had hot-wired a car and stolen it from a pub car park with the intention of selling it in London. But he was stopped driving south on the A1 after filling up with petrol and not paying for it.

The ex-Eagles reserve also admitted a variety of offences in London. He stole a bottle of spirits and a computer game but was spotted by a store detective.

Langham, of St David's Drive, Scawsby, Doncaster, admitted robbery, burglary, thefts and assault and was jailed for three years and ten months.

Defending, Tim Savage said Langham had since become drug free, had gained star qualifications as a Rugby League and gymnasium coach from which he "hoped to make a living and intended staying away from crime".

Eagles chief executive Ralph Rimmer said: "It's sad to see a lad with a lot of ability wasted. He certainly did have a lot of talent."

Chapter 11

MIXING WITH THE "MAFIA"

I came back from court with mixed emotions. I had not become a long-term prisoner – only just – but still had a substantial time to serve. There was relief from all the anxiety that had built up; a weight had dropped off my shoulders. But I was still on 23-hour lock-up in the segregation unit. Next morning I was given an hour to pack my kit; they couldn't wait to get rid of me. I was being "ghosted" onto a plain white bus, which meant I was not told where I was being taken. And I was the only passenger. At any given moment there are scores of convicts being transported up and down Britain's motorways, a fact which has the added useful effect of temporarily freeing up space in the nation's crowded prisons. My worst fear was that I would end up on the Isle of Wight, which is notorious for hosting violent prisoners. I was classed as one of them, and I could soon tell from the road signs that I was indeed heading south.

The journey took ages, but eventually we drove up to the gates of HMP Wandsworth, a forbidding old Victorian prison in south London. It was a big culture shock, as what I had sampled so far were relatively cushy numbers. There were no frills here and I was duly kitted out in a proper striped shirt along with a pair of jeans that were far too big. The next thing I knew, I was queuing up for tea with my metal tray when the riot alarm went off. In the ensuing pandemonium, chased by prison officers wielding truncheons, we were all locked up, and I never got any tea. Nor did I ever discover what had caused the problem.

My stay would be very short. At six o'clock the following morning I was told I was going to nearby Brixton prison. That was another shock, as I discovered I was the only white person in the whole of the reception wing – I was a bit racist in those days.

The weekends there were tough because we were hardly let out of our cells, I guess through staff shortage as much as anything. In my early days there I suffered two long weekends owing to bank holidays, which are among the most horrendous memories I have: over those two weekends there were nine suicides. It wasn't just the tragedy of inmates being so depressed that they should take their own lives, but the degrading way in which their sad demise was treated. You would hear the zip of the body bags followed by the plonking of the heavy weight as they were dragged down the metal steps by a single officer, all of which created an increasingly hostile environment. All went quiet and eerie as the ghoulish noise echoed through the wing, and our hearts would be pounding, wondering who it was.

I was surrounded by dangerous gangsters from all kinds of backgrounds – Cockneys from the East End, Chinese Triads, Rastafarians, Greek Cypriots – all having bags of money and power on the outside and involved in multi-million-pound drug cartels. Corruption was rife, as their contacts soon got to know where to locate off-duty officers – at their regular pub, for instance – and blackmail, in the interests of drug-running and the like, was the inevitable result. They even managed to smuggle in prostitutes disguised as legal assistants. So it wasn't surprising the place was flooded with drugs and was under investigation at the time.

My first cellmate was a Cockney who never seemed to stop talking, mostly in the rhyming slang which so characterizes the East End of London. So when he asked me if I wanted any "Holy Ghost", I thought at first he was into religion until I realized he was offering me some toast. And did I want a "cup of Rosie Lee" (tea)? I just sat there with my mouth open, listening to him tell me how he had mixed with the notorious Kray brothers – he was quite a name-dropper, and prison life was second nature to him.

Fortunately, by this time I was officially detoxed from heroin (a process that typically takes about a week), and had been clean for about nine months. After two days I was offered a cleaning job, which kept me out of the cell much of the time and qualified me for certain privileges, such as getting clothes that fitted, nice food, and even the occasional luxury like chocolates (from my prison officer boss). Prisoners are always craving food because it's a kind of slop they serve. I settled into the routine pretty easily and, because of my job, was spending up to twelve hours a day with officers, which is bound to have an effect. The days of not fraternizing with staff were a thing of the past thanks to an incentive scheme which awarded certain privileges – like early release and extra visits – for passing on useful information.

I was eating well and training at the gym every day and had everything I needed. But I was hundreds of miles from home, and my family didn't want to know me any more. I started doing some correspondence courses and writing a lot of letters – to Bonnie, my sisters, and friends, people I thought I had let down. I was very emotional – a common side effect of coming off heroin, as the drug suppresses emotion – and began to think clearly. I started looking into philosophy and, for the first time, started to ask the questions: "Who am I? What am I doing here? Is there a supreme being? What about the Big Bang?" I did a lot of reading and was enthralled by various people's views and opinions. I was reading nearly a book a day at one point. And so time passed.

One day I found a pile of letters on my bed. It was like Christmas! Some were from solicitors, but friends and family had started writing back too. This included Bonnie, who sent a heartfelt forty-page letter telling me all about Emily and enclosed a photo of her. I replied many times but never got another response. However, that one letter and picture of my baby daughter got me through that sentence. I hung it on the wall, and it helped me focus on getting myself right as I educated myself by correspondence in philosophy, Buddhism, yoga – all sorts – clocking up a total of forty-six qualifications, spurred on by that photograph of Emily.

Meantime, earlier offences which had not previously come to light were now coming out of the woodwork, such as giving a false name when nicked during my homeless days, which risked adding to my sentence. I was also called to give evidence at the trial of a police officer who had assaulted me during one of my arrests (he was "grassed" by a colleague who witnessed the incident, and I had forgotten about it). I was then ghosted back to Doncaster to answer a charge for a relatively menial offence, and it was like a holiday. I walked straight back onto the wing from which I had been dragged off for failing a drug test. A month later I was returned to Brixton to give evidence at the police officer's appeal hearing, which he lost.

From there I was immediately bundled into a van and taken to Belmarsh prison – one of Britain's top security institutions where some inmates were so high risk they were incarcerated in a "prison within the prison". I mixed with lifers, terrorists, Triads, and gangsters, with a Godfather figure taking me under his wing. Most of the prisoners were serving at least twenty years for such things as murder and armed robbery. I have never experienced such violence and aggression; it was an intensely volatile cauldron of unpredictability always on the verge of exploding. There was a real heaviness in the atmosphere, and the officers were merely puppets. I had put on a lot of weight – a mixture of muscle and fat – and was known as "Yorkshire Pudding".

Because I felt I had to be as ruthless as the people around me in that environment, I became more aggressive. I witnessed gang-rapes, and some of the prisoners even paid for sex with transgender people who were in a men's prison because they still had male organs. It was a very dangerous place, seething with depravity, and inmates had to watch their back every minute of the day, preferably armed with home-made weapons. I was completely out of my depth, and yet I could get on with people because I was a sociable type. I made friends with this lonely old guy (or so I thought) who turned out to be a ruthless gangster and got very close with another chap called Ronnie who was doing fifteen years for armed robbery. The three of us hung out all the time.

At the same time I kept up my training, as I genuinely got immersed in trying to better myself. I got a well-paid job (£40 a week) packing lightbulbs and started going to church. I got drawn to the chapel, perhaps through loneliness, but also following the calling to the spiritual side of things I'd always felt, even as a boy going to church in Scawsby. When my mum died, I turned away from all the positive things, including church, and started to replace them with negatives like drink and drugs. But whenever that has been stripped away, I've always been led back to where I'm meant to be, with God.

I even started praying for other prisoners, guided by the prison chaplains. When I was praying for another prisoner, for a split second I didn't feel like a prisoner myself. I had a role. It wasn't just about me. I had lived a completely selfish life, and here was an act that was completely unselfish.

It wasn't just me – there was some kind of a revival going on in the prison at the time, with inmates committing their lives to Jesus. A newspaper at the time published an editorial headed "There is an answer to the drugs dilemma!" It included the following statement: "Anglican prison chaplain David Powe, currently based at Belmarsh in south-east London, is seeing hundreds of criminals find real purpose to their lives through the 'Powe-r' of the gospel."

This chaplain prayed over me in a strange language, which I thought was Latin at the time but have since realized was more likely to have been tongues, the language given by the Holy Spirit when normal words seem inadequate. I remember feeling fuzzy, like I had been electrocuted. My heart was pounding. I've no doubt a seed was sown with some sort of helpful spiritual impartation. I was obviously at Belmarsh for this reason. I shouldn't have been there really as it was a high-security establishment, and I wasn't categorized as such.

I then became pals with a Greek Cypriot who was getting heroin into prison, and I started dabbling with the drug again. But as contact from home increased and the dynamics of the prison began to change, I started to hanker after going back up north. A paedophile came on the wing for having raped a toddler and got stabbed, though he did survive. My friends were moved elsewhere and I was becoming increasingly fearful, having to watch my back all the more.

So I was ecstatic when I was eventually transferred back to Moorland prison on the outskirts of Doncaster two days before Christmas 1999. As we left London in the van, I swore I never wanted to see the place again. It was definitely a case of "Get me out of here!" I had witnessed the horrors of homelessness, crack and heroin addiction, sexual abuse, ever-present violence, and shocking suicides. I resolved I was definitely going to turn over a new leaf the following year and finally sort myself out.

Another shock was in store, as I had to start working my way towards jobs and privileges all over again at a new place. I started to wonder why I had pushed for the move as I saw in the new millennium behind bars. On the plus side, I received my first family visit for a year and even got an airmail letter from my dad, saying he wanted to get back into my life. He was now living in the south of Ireland with his partner Hilary. I felt I was back home, even if I had picked up something of a Cockney accent.

I eventually settled down at Moorland and it was there that I completed most of the forty-six courses I took – among them English and Maths GCSEs, sport and recreation, and coaching and refereeing for all kinds of sports, including volleyball. I also gained an industrial cleaning certificate, coached and played for the rugby union team, and became the gym orderly, which perfectly fitted my training regime. My NVQ (National Vocational Qualification) trainer and assessor, John Potter, was a born-again Christian who was always eating raw carrots (he was a vegetarian).

Having been drug-free at Moorland for about ten months, I set up a peer mentoring group to help others come off substances. I had become a different person and my head was filled with all kinds of philosophy. I had started reading Christian literature, including a book called *Conversations with God* by Neale Donald Walsch, but I also explored Buddhism and meditation. I would go to chapel on Sunday, but also attend a Buddhism class. I was searching for God, as are most prisoners, if they're honest. When that cell door shuts on you for the first time, every single prisoner cries and questions what life is all about.

On the downside, the chip on my shoulder wasn't getting any smaller as I reverted to my aggressive behaviour, lashing out at whoever crossed me, which only had the effect of adding further time to my sentence. I started threatening staff and ended up in a fight, first on the wing and then by knocking someone out on the football pitch – apparently a classic symptom of the fear of approaching release, not knowing what to expect in the outside world, with an uncertain future and a blot against your name leaving job prospects difficult, to say the least. I was determined to show the world I was no smackhead, and I wanted my daughter and girlfriend back. With rippling muscles and shaved head, I looked pretty mean. But I was mixed up mentally and emotionally, with a very distorted view of life. I had witnessed things I never hope to see again. I was a seventeen-stone ticking time bomb with a massive chip on my shoulder, and in that parlous state was released back into the community in January 2001.

I had entered prison as a nineteen-year-old teenager and come out a very different person, aged twenty-two. I was seriously disturbed. After initially staying with Catherine, and then my friend Cliff, I was reconciled with Bonnie and, for a six-month honeymoon period, was living a normal life, training and playing rugby, car valeting, working as a nightclub bouncer, and enjoying restored relationships with my sisters. Emily was now three and I was seeing her for the first time. I was initially playing rugby union at Rawmarsh, after being introduced through my contact at Moorland. Then I got back with my old Rugby League club, now known (temporarily, as it turned out) as Doncaster Dragons, turning out for their

Alliance (academy) team for the 2001–2 season. At last there was some sort of structure to my life and, by the end of April, I was back in the *Star*, this time in a much more positive light under the headline "SECOND CHANCE" in the paper's Doncaster edition. David Kessen reported:

Doncaster rugby star Allen Langham today opened the lid on a drugs hell he has finally conquered after a long battle.

The 23-year-old has beaten heroin addiction and returned to playing professional rugby league with Doncaster Dragons.

Opening his heart to the Doncaster Star, he said he is delighted to have been given a second chance in the game and in life. He hopes his story will stop anyone else from slipping into the twilight world of drugs which landed him with a four-year prison sentence in 1999.

For Allen, his shocking story began when he found himself behind bars following a nightclub brawl. At the time he had been an emerging youngster with Sheffield Eagles, then a Super League side. His contract was cancelled and, after he left prison, he planned to take a year out of the game to start a sports management business.

But back on the streets of Doncaster he met up with a former fellow inmate who introduced him to heroin.

"Before I knew what was happening I was on a downward slope. I always thought I was better than that," says Allen, of Scawsby.

"But it is really easy to get addicted to heroin. You always think you're in control. I knew what heroin was and what it had done to people, but I didn't believe that could happen to me. I had money and material things and thought I was different to other users. Before I knew it the addiction was there."

Allen believes it was prison which saved him in the end.

In June 1999 he was sent to prison for a catalogue of stealing offences, including burglary and robbery. And it was at that point he pulled himself together and began to beat his addiction, concentrating on getting himself back to fitness. He had a picture on his wall of his baby daughter, who was growing up while he was behind bars, to remind him of why he must sort his life out.

He returned to the sport after being released early and was soon playing rugby union for Rawmarsh (near Rotherham). And this season he is back with Doncaster Dragons where he first started his rugby league career as a teenage academy player. He is grateful to the club and his family for standing by him. He has been clear of drugs for two-and-a-half years now, but still takes things a day at a time.

"My sisters Catherine and Rosemary have been diamonds throughout," he said. "They listened, arranged for me to see counsellors, always stood by me and never gave up on me when I nearly gave up on myself.

"Luckily Doncaster Dragons have given me a second

chance, and I've played as a substitute for the last few games. It's still a battle, but now I have so much going for me. I'm enjoying seeing my daughter grow up, I have good people around me and I have rugby and work. Now I just want to stop anyone else going down the wrong road."

However, all was not as well as it seemed. I had a good season with the Dragons but, although finally clean of heroin and crack, I was still using a heady mixture of cocaine and alcohol, and going out drinking with the lads. There was so much unresolved stuff in my mixed-up life. I was full of rage and resentment. I tried so many times to sort myself out and turn my life around; it certainly wasn't for want of trying that I failed each time. I was determined to shake off the smackhead stigma now attached to me, but the old self-destructive nature would soon rear its ugly head again as I vented the fury built up from a lifetime of pain, hurt, and mistrust, and I was soon getting involved in punch-ups like before and basking in the adulation of being a hardman who had done time in prison with heavy-duty gangsters.

I also got into trouble on the pitch when I struck out at a referee while playing in an amateur capacity for Doncaster Toll Bar in Division 1 of the Yorkshire League. Apparently I was only going to be shown a yellow card but then I swore at the ref, Nigel Burrows, who duly produced a red card. The next thing he knew he was being attended to by medics on the pitch. He suffered a broken nose and a pair of black eyes for his trouble, having already had his jaw broken by another player in an earlier match. The game was abandoned with Toll Bar leading 18–14. I was banned from the club, and received a life ban as a player from the Rugby League headquarters. It felt worse than a prison term. I was spiralling out of control once more.

Chapter 12

ON THE RUN

Before the storm, however, it was all relatively calm. I was in a good place for a while – working, training hard, playing rugby, and rediscovering a home life with my girlfriend and child. But I suppose I was drinking pretty heavily, though this was generally restricted to twice-weekly binges. It was a happy time for me, having emerged from the hell of heroin and prison. I was often cooking big meals for people and was starting to turn our house into a home. But drinking sparked off dramas between us, and I was very protective of Bonnie when out drinking in a pub, threatening anyone who so much as looked at her.

When I began mixing cocaine with alcohol as we partied away towards the end of the rugby season, I was on the slippery slope. Bonnie resented me for having left her at her time of greatest need, when she was pregnant, and for having missed Emily's birth due to being behind bars. She was hurting and felt betrayed whereas I was jealous and insecure, and we started to argue. Whereas at first we were soulmates madly in love, I had changed because of my experiences and I was no longer the big friendly guy she had fallen in love with.

Then one day I caught her in a compromising embrace with Frank, my best friend. Frank and I had literally grown up with each other and were inseparable, even going on holidays together. In one moment, my entire life seemed to collapse around me. I jumped in the car and drove off. I was in shock, weeping with pain I hadn't felt since my mum's death. In one fell swoop I had lost my partner, daughter, and best friend.

Looking back, it was one more consequence of going down the drug trail. When I returned, I shoved Bonnie out of my way and then handed Frank a knockout blow when he stepped in to defend her. As she screamed in my face, with every word like another knife stabbing me, I punched her. And when Frank came to her defence again, I battered him to within half an inch of his life as he lay gasping for breath on the floor. It was probably the most severe beating I'd ever handed out. It was the classic case of love turning to hate. Bonnie was left with a black eye, and Frank disfigured. Later, I cried when I saw the state I'd reduced Frank to. He begged me not to tell his girlfriend what had happened. I reckoned things couldn't get any worse, so I went out to a rave and got absolutely hammered with drink, in the process of which I got involved in about ten fights before winding up at a friend's house in nearby Balby.

The entire motivation for getting off heroin and out of prison had been to get my partner and daughter back. Now that was all over, everything started to deteriorate. Everyone fell out with me as I went on the rampage, glassing someone in a pub. At the same time, Billy, my mentor of earlier days, died of a heart attack while working on a roof, and I took his son Gaz under my wing. He was as volatile as me. By this time I was moving large amounts of cannabis, but, as soon as I had drunk too much, I would get upset and start looking for a fight. My level of violence intensified and I began to collect drug debts and got paid to break people's legs. I started to sleep around and kept being arrested for harassment. Although I knew it was over with Bonnie, I couldn't resist the temptation of going back there to make trouble. Naturally, in view of the way I handled things, I lost custody of Emily. I was in such a mess again, so disorientated with life.

Meanwhile, Gaz wrapped my car around a lamppost, yet emerged unscathed, and I started an affair with his sister. Then I visited a pub where Bonnie's dad drank and, when the landlord refused to serve me, I picked up an ashtray and threw it, leaving him with a serious head injury. I made a quick getaway and caused further mayhem in town, laying out four nightclub bouncers in the process. But when I realized the police were on my trail, I decided to go on the run… to Ireland, where my dad lived.

I was duly treated to a "going away" party at the Sun Inn, Scawsby, at which friends chipped in towards my fare. Although feeling as rough as a badger from all the booze and fighting, and owing thousands in drug money which I left my friend Cliff to sort out, I took the train to Holyhead on the west coast of Wales, where I caught the ferry to Dublin.

When I got there I phoned my dad from a call box, and discovered that Enniscorthy, where he lived, was hours away. So I caught a bus, finally meeting him for the first time as a grown-up. I had decided I was going to start a new life out there. But almost immediately after my arrival, he and his partner Hilary left for a pre-booked holiday in Cork, leaving me to fend for myself with 100 euros and some food, having introduced me to a cousin with a broad Irish accent. He was worse than me. He only needed two pints before wanting to fight everybody, and we soon got into some serious scrapes involving punch-ups with bouncers and German tourists, and me kicking the door of a pub which had refused us entry. The Garda (police) were eventually called out, but the really scary part was when a beat-up old car pulled up alongside us and the driver told me: "You're as good as dead, Blue Nose." I subsequently found out that "Blue Nose" was a nickname for a Protestant, and that I had been given a classic IRA warning. It meant the IRA were going to kill me, I was told, and the area was an IRA stronghold.

I had only been there forty-eight hours when I realized I needed to get out of Ireland as fast as I had got out of Doncaster. Having spent all my money on Guinness and beer, I called my sister in desperation, and she booked a ferry from Belfast. When I explained that was like jumping from the frying pan into the fire – it was another IRA stronghold – my booking was switched to Dublin. And three days after leaving the Sun Inn in a shower of champagne with everyone contributing towards my new life, I was back there with my tail between my legs getting dirty looks. But they ended up laughing their heads off as it turned into a "welcome home" party.

Within two days I was charged with malicious wounding and, surprisingly, bailed, provided I could live out of town away from Bonnie. I found myself a bedsit in Sprotbrough, a pleasant village on the west of town. But it wasn't a safe place for me as it was there that I got involved with Marco, who came from a family of grave-robbers and was involved in the distribution of a quality Dutch weed known as skunk. I was drawn into his web like a puppet on a string as I ran up drug debts and began mixing with serious criminals in Barnsley who were involved in drug-running operations at various locations.

At one point I got hold of a cache of ecstasy and Viagra from an Asian connection. I swallowed a mouthful of it and was soon out of my face, attacking the television, chucking it out of the window and then going down the road with it as if I was walking a dog. The police were alerted, but took one look at me and scarpered.

It was around the time of the 2002 World Cup that I decided, rather as the mafia do, that I would invest the illicit money we were making in legitimate business. I hit on the idea of purchasing a load of English memorabilia from a Doncaster guy known as One-eyed Lennie, a barrel of a man with a glass eye who had about ten phones going simultaneously and would light his next fag with the one he was already smoking. And so, armed with flags, caps, T-shirts, and the like, we would set up stalls at markets on the east and west coasts. But my business flair wasn't up to much, and it was with a view to extricating ourselves from the ever-deepening hole of debt caused by drugs and dodgy deals that we hired a Ford Ka for a trip to Amsterdam. It was comical, with four of us – all big, hunky men – crammed into this tiny vehicle for what turned out to be a twenty-six-hour drive via Dover and the Cross-Channel Ferry.

We were on a mission to buy a kilo of skunk, which could be bought from Dutch coffee shops in small amounts, but by the time we had done with spending most of the money on a pub crawl, along with touring the "sin city" bursting at the seams with show girls and lap dancers, we only had enough for half a kilo – worth about £3,000 on the street. And that was a struggle because the Dutch were loath to do deals with the English. Money was also wasted by taking a wrong turning on the way there, finding ourselves within sight of the German Alps.

When we returned to Calais to board the ferry back home, we had prepared ourselves with fake evidence of job interviews showing that we were labourers and bricklayers seeking work. But just as my friend Jody and I were about to board the ferry, the other two said they were taking the hovercraft, and it suddenly dawned on us that they were using us as mules.

We must have looked like two of the shadiest characters, and the most inept drug smugglers, that Customs officers have ever seen, with half a kilo of weed stuffed down our pants. But because we had not travelled abroad before, and were not known as drug smugglers, they restricted their search to the car, which we had carefully stripped of any incriminating evidence. It was a close thing. Jody went very pale when we were directed to pull aside for inspection. Although I tried hard to act normally, my legs were shaking and my feet were on the pedals, ready for a swift take-off as soon as the gates opened.

It was about this time I met Steph, the mother of my second daughter Alice. She was model material, and had just returned from running a bar with her sister in Gran Canaria.

Chapter 13

WATCHING MY BABY'S BIRTH

I guess I had been looking to fill the gap left by the split with Bonnie, and I was strongly attracted to Steph, a twin with bleached blonde hair and an immaculate figure. We began life together on Marco's living room floor, where we shared a mattress and became inseparable. She was a female version of me, having once been charged with grievous bodily harm and having beaten someone up on another occasion with her high-heeled shoe. We then moved into her mum's, where we had our own room. Those first months together were beautiful. Although she found it hard to show love, she was loyal and faithful, and never made me feel jealous or insecure.

Meanwhile, my court case for the malicious wounding charge was looming. Fully expecting me to get sent down, we decided on a farewell celebration at a pub in Mexborough, halfway between Barnsley and

Doncaster, the night before I was due to appear for sentencing. Afterwards we retreated to my old friend Cliff's place for what turned into a wild party complete with cocaine. Cliff was in an aggressive mood for some reason, and when he discovered me urinating outside the back door, proceeded to kick me where it hurts most. He then tried out his ju-jitsu on me, holding me down while others joined in the fracas, during which I managed to snap Gaz's finger. Once I had managed to extricate myself from Cliff's martial arts grip, I really laid into him and we slugged it out for the next forty-five minutes. The police were called, but, when they noticed who was fighting, they got straight back in their car and drove off. I eventually had my foot on Cliff's head but, because of my love for him, couldn't bring myself to finish the job. So I was sporting cuts, bruises, and black eyes in court next day, which was explained away as a rugby injury. The prosecution accepted my guilty plea and agreed that no malice was intended, so I was given two years' probation and a £750 fine.

I continued living in a drug-induced, delusional world of little reality, which had the effect of diffusing the mounting pressure on a life falling to pieces. Steph had announced that she wanted a baby before she was twenty-five and duly became pregnant. We moved into a council house in Worsbrough Common, overlooking a lovely valley, and I remember thinking how I could have settled there forever.

We started decorating our home while I worked a twelve-hour shift at Sainsbury's an hour's drive away to the south of Sheffield. But Steph was on an emotional roller coaster – she was sick all through her pregnancy – and without any warning one day upped sticks and moved in with her mum, swapping kitchen units she had just bought for baby paraphernalia. With our relationship on and off throughout this time, I was in limbo in more ways than one – also selling skunk on the one hand and trying to go straight on the other.

Then I made another bad decision. Noticing a couple of youths breaking in next door, I gave them both a good bashing, only to discover they were sons of heavy-duty mean men from the area. Soon afterwards I saw three hooded men marching towards me with what looked like bats in their hands, and another coming from the opposite direction as they closed in on me. I instinctively turned around and took on the lone guy, levelled him to the ground with a punch, and ran off to Marco's, throwing up all over the place when he opened the door as fear tightened its grip on me. When I got back to the house next morning, the whole place had been smashed up, as well as my car. I had bitten off more than I could chew. Now I had nowhere to live with a baby on the way, though Steph's mum took pity on me and took me in.

Steph was heavily into praying to angels. We would sit together in the front room at her mum's and receive readings of cards. It was fortune-telling – dangerous ground to be on, even if it did, ultimately and weirdly, lead me to Christ by introducing me to the spiritual realm. Angels now camp around me! When I became born again, I thanked Steph – though I made it clear I had taken a different direction and was a born-again believer.

Meanwhile, I was rapidly heading for a mental breakdown – living with constant fear of reprisals, thousands of pounds in debt to drug barons and now with some really mean gangsters after my head. I was drowning in a swamp of stress, negative emotion, cannabis, and drink. I was beginning to have some strange experiences, such as seeing a "spirit" coming out of Steph when arguing with her on one occasion. I was seeing things on the TV that weren't there.

I eventually found a place for us to rent, and, as a thank you to friends for helping me decorate, I took them out to a pub in Bentley, Doncaster, called The Drum, which was heaving with people I had crossed swords with. When I headbutted one of them, half the pub turned on me. I needed to get out fast but my friend Jody was standing in front of my car with his hands in the air, shouting, "Stop!" I sent him flying into the air (yes, I could have killed him, but fortunately he didn't even need hospital treatment), and when I got back to Barnsley Steph's mum wouldn't let me in. (Our house wasn't yet ready for moving in.) So I took out my frustration on an innocent man passing by, although I imagined at the time he was saying something derogatory to me. A street battle ensued, during which I bit his finger and ear, but he was too proud to give up and kept coming at me. The police were waiting for me at the bottom of the road and I was arrested. I woke up in their cells, denying any offence, though they had been told my victim had been "savaged like a dog".

After starting yet another fracas, I received death threats, which finally tipped me over the edge into total mental breakdown. I went to the doctor, who referred me for specialist treatment, and was diagnosed with Acute Predominantly Delusional Disorder, for which I was given tablets along with a plan to help ease off my alcohol consumption. Once again, I had hit rock bottom. I was a write-off – people were laughing at me. I had lost all my bottle; I was just a wreck. But I was having counselling sessions with a support agency in Barnsley, who were really helping me, and I started to make a gradual recovery.

Charged with serious assault, I made the mistake of insisting on pleading not guilty, which meant the case going for trial at Sheffield Crown Court.

On 8 January 2004, meanwhile, Alice was born. Something inside me softened that day. I was the first person to see her; I cut the cord. I dropped to the floor and cried like a baby, but they were tears of joy. I remember saying how she even had my funny web-like toes. And in that special moment I loved Steph; I was so proud of her. She had suffered three days of labour and yet still looked so beautiful. I arranged for a limousine to pick her up from the hospital. All the family came along and she was given a champagne reception – a memory I will cherish for the rest of my life. Looking back, I felt it was the start of my journey of salvation. I wanted to rectify the mistakes I had made when I first became a father. I'd been given a second chance and was starting to rebuild my life. Oh yes, I had serious mental health issues – I was angry, volatile, unpredictable, and a dangerous career criminal – but I had turned a corner. Alice was now everything to me, and I would spend hours each day watching over her.

None of the senior barristers would take me on because of my stubbornness in insisting on pleading not guilty, so I was lumbered with a guy from London who didn't do me any favours. The three-day trial finished with the jury deliberating for forty-five minutes and coming up with a unanimous guilty verdict for actual bodily harm. I was sentenced to three years and three months which, with good behaviour, worked out at nineteen and a half months whereas, if I had pleaded guilty, I would probably have been out of prison in six months. Now I was looking at a long separation from my newborn baby, and I was devastated. Steph broke down in court, and I was shell-shocked.

So, in the summer of 2004 I was once again being driven back to Doncaster's Marsh Gate prison, knowing I wasn't going to see daylight for another two years. I sobbed my heart out all the way back from Sheffield. I had a missus and a baby, and now I was torn away from them.

The pills I'd been given for my psychiatric problems were almost knocking me unconscious – I had stopped taking them earlier because of this effect, but now had to take my medicine in front of the officers. I literally slept off the weed and alcohol for the first three weeks, and eventually had enough energy to resume my gym workouts. The mental health team in the prison were amazing. A Community Psychiatric Nurse was assigned to me, and my mixed-up mind gradually straightened out with the help of therapy so that I was grateful for being there in the end.

I was getting regular visits from my little family. I was moved to Lindholme prison on the outskirts of town (near Moorland) where my rugby background worked in my favour as I became the gym officer's orderly. The next eight months was a time of pure blessing! Mind you, things very nearly got off to a bad start when I saw a photo on the wall of my first cell of some guys I had beaten up a while back, which included my new cellmate. He kept saying he had seen me before, but couldn't quite place me. I knew who he was all right, but we made up and became very good friends.

Then I was moved to another wing which accommodated the guy who had stabbed my teenage friend Carl to death some years earlier. I wanted to smash his head in, and was just about to grab an opportunity to do so when an officer saw me. It was a saving grace, for the next day the man was moved onto the lifer's wing, where he was almost immediately beaten up. I know it sounds odd now, but I was afterwards able to bask in the glory of avenging my friend's death without having done the deed, letting my mates think I was the culprit – though of course I'm glad I didn't do it. I subsequently got to know him, and for the first time in my life began to feel genuine compassion for someone. Wracked with guilt, he became a chronic heroin user. He told me he had never meant to kill my friend – just inflict an injury to frighten him.

In the meantime, I learnt new skills, studied for more qualifications, and taught fellow inmates how to train. I was then moved to nearby Hatfield, an open prison with a very laid-back regime and lots of privileges, such as regular visits to town. But I had to serve another two months before I could qualify for these outings. As had so often been the case, I had no patience and was going stir crazy. So I reverted to my self-destruct mode in a foolish bid to be seen as the boyo macho man, duly arranging for a parcel of drugs, spirits, food, mobile phones, and even a duvet to be dropped off by one of the visitors. Unfortunately the prison was renowned for its informants and I subsequently failed a drug test – in fact, I blew the scale. I was moved to Moorland, not far away, having completely blown the chance of regular home visits for want of behaving myself just a little longer.

I confessed all to Steph, who refused to continue her visits, which at least gave me a fresh incentive to get sorted, especially when I saw the cutting of my *Doncaster Star* "second chance" story pinned on the gym wall. The staff there were devastated that I was back behind bars, and, as the cold light of day hit me like a sledgehammer, I threw myself into the gym and education – even taking a course in driving a forklift truck – and resolved to quit drinking. But I have to say that Steph's mum Linda was totally loyal, visiting me every week, for which I am very grateful.

Meanwhile, I was spiritually searching. I would never say I always believed in God, but I always believed in something – I just wasn't sure what that something was. I've sat in Mormon and spiritualist meetings, I've gone to séances, I've had crystals on me – always searching for that one thing. In prison, I got heavily into Buddhism, thinking I'd find the answer through meditation. I learned about Hinduism from a guy I shared a cell with, but was convinced I could see evil in his eyes. So I had now started to pray, but without really knowing who I was praying to. And once again I attended chapel too. Every single prison sentence, I think I've always ended up back in the chapel, or in some kind of service.

I attended an Alcoholics Anonymous group, which is a twelve-step course based on Christian principles, and some of those with whom I shared my problems were Christians. I wasn't addicted to alcohol as such, but it acted as the fuel releasing my unpredictable and violent behaviour, which is why I was happy to be referred to them. Meanwhile I became fit and strong, coached rugby, and took part in a rowing, cycling, and running triathlon for charity. A prison officer called Pete really put his neck on the line for me, and I am so grateful to him.

I did eventually qualify for regular home leaves, and fell on my feet on release from prison when Steph's dad, an engineer based in Indonesia, loaned us the money to buy a three-storey town house on a brand new estate in the Barnsley district of Kendray. Alice was two and a half by now. I was soon signed off from mental health cover. I became a gym instructor for a special needs project and was accepted at Hillsborough College in Sheffield for a foundation degree in sports coaching and exercise science. Things were really looking up. But it seemed that every time I got myself to a good place in life, I pressed the self-destruct button. It was preceded by a honeymoon period which saw me playing rugby again with the Dons (known as the Lakers at this time) for the 2006–7 season, but unresolved personal issues once more took over my life as I became embroiled in a cocktail of drink, drugs, and illicit dealing.

Chapter 14

BLOOD-CURDLING HORROR

While I was in a much better frame of mind, I was seen as this chap who always had a big heart for people, taking on their problems, even fighting on their behalf, standing up for their causes. But as I once again found myself caught in the vicious circle of drugs, I started to develop a form of obsessive compulsive disorder (OCD), especially with cleanliness around the house. Part of this was because I was still mentally in prison, with all its routines. I became obsessed with time – while inside, I would set myself targets, like seeing my stretch in terms of, say, a dozen visits left, or taking up an eight-week gym course which would account for two months' stir. It all helped to get through the sentence. But for the most part I tended to rebel against all that structure as soon as I got released, which is why I generally went wild after a honeymoon of peace and tranquillity, living a chaotic life.

I was getting paid handsomely for organizing drug deals, and used it to set myself up in the business of buying and selling cars. I virtually became a house husband for a time, looking after Alice, cooking, and keeping the place spic and span. Then I bumped into an old contact who was able to source a potent variety of cocaine, and I became a middleman again. I felt I had to keep buying expensive items like new boots for Steph to prove my love. After two years apart we had both become different people. So now I was smoking cannabis and dabbling in cocaine but trying to keep off the booze while obsessively cleaning the house to avoid arguments when Steph got home. We were both insecure, vulnerable people who had been let down in the past. Keeping her in a good mood became a daily battle, and we argued and fought – her strongest weapon being words. We were constantly bickering and I finally snapped, dragging her out of the house by her hair!

Marco was there to witness this tirade, and it had such a profound effect on him that he has not touched a drop of alcohol since or involved himself in any more dodgy deals. He called it his "epiphany" or "moment of clarity" and became a new man; he's now the boss of a legitimate scaffolding company.

These people in Barnsley had reintroduced me to the idea of family. It could be somewhere I belonged. But the lifestyle I was living was just too dangerous. Steph's twin Barbie was worried that I'd end up killing her sister. To my shame, they had every reason to be afraid of me. I got into further trouble with Steph, kicking her door in out of frustration at not being let in. And I was soon on the wanted list again, but managed to evade the police despite having CS gas sprayed into my face. I went back to Ireland to see my dad but had little quality time with him, as I was constantly on the phone trying to sort out the mess I had created. But I found some peace in a small village church, where I prayed for help.

I returned on Christmas Eve when the all-clear was given on account of statements against me having been withdrawn. Unfortunately the festivities turned into a disaster with drunken arguments, and I walked out on New Year's Day 2007. We had both had enough. We separated and I soon rejoined the roller coaster ride of drinking, fighting, and taking drugs. Despite that, I set up a plastering company and was given permission to move back to Doncaster. At any rate I was determined to maintain regular contact with Alice. There were subsequent attempts to patch things up with Steph and I got into further scuffles in my bid to retrieve my own possessions from the house, demanding to have everything back I had bought. On one such occasion I gave chase to her new boyfriend, pulling off his car's wing mirror in the process.

I finally moved back to my home town, where I hadn't lived for five years, and where my reputation had become legend, with younger lads putting me on a pedestal. I was a superhero in their eyes, and played up to it. They would say: "I expected you to be nine foot tall and five foot wide, but you're actually a nice guy!" And women would throw themselves at me because I was this big, hard man. With a bachelor pad in the suburb of Lakeside complete with balcony and a view of the lake, I played the field – not on the nearby Rugby League ground as I should have done, but among the women of the town. With money still fluid, though not legitimate of course, I wore the best clothes and aftershave. But at the same time I was a good dad with Alice at weekends. My spiritual quest had taken a temporary back seat as I went all materialistic, but I didn't find any happiness with it. I was sleeping around with stunning women and waking up feeling dirty. I had always been a relationship man, but now I didn't want to commit myself to anyone. If anybody tried to get close, I'd push them away. There was no trust, respect or love; it was only about satisfying my insatiable sexual appetite. It was just a matter of wining and dining, and getting into bed. I became addicted to sex. A certain type of woman is attracted to the hard man; they enjoy the danger because it's a kind of adventure.

Meanwhile, the plastering firm had morphed into a building company, and we had just made £10,000 profit on an extension. I got back into a close relationship with Cliff, the gentle giant with whom I'd had that terrible fight. But he was deteriorating mentally. He had built up a property empire but was mortgaged to the hilt, and the boom was starting to collapse. In addition, he had been tempted into sexual deviancy, drink, cocaine, brothels, and orgies amid questions over his sexuality. I believe he had split-personality issues. He became a cage fighter, and was taking hormones and steroids. There were also family problems – for example, his wealthy dad left his mum and got involved with a much younger woman – and family was very important to him. He started to self-harm and was found at the bottom of the stairs with a huge gash in his arm. Because he had always been the one who told everyone else what to do, no one felt able to intervene.

Even with my apparently glittering hedonistic lifestyle – the sex, drink, drugs, parties, clothes, and jewellery – I was empty and alone. I had some serious bouts of depression, even though the construction business was picking up nicely. I also took up golf, hacking my way around a course at Owston, just north of the town.

Then came Mother's Day 2008, by which time I had moved back to Scawsby, where I'd grown up, and was living there for the first time since some vigilantes had banned me from the area ten years earlier. It was just after my thirtieth birthday, and we were nursing the effects of an all-night binge. Cliff knocked on the door around breakfast time asking for a drink. We got through a bottle of vodka while he poured his heart out to me, telling me how he had tried to end his life and showing me a big scar on his wrist. Though a successful businessman, he couldn't live with what he had become. His mum was very poorly, and he was in a mess. But he promised me not to harm himself again.

Then it dawned on me that it was Mother's Day... and the death of my mum sixteen years earlier suddenly hit me with the emotional force of a hurricane. There was nothing for it but to go on another binge, causing mayhem in different pubs and ending up smashing the tables and chairs at one particular hostelry, for which I would receive a suspended sentence. We started at the Newton, where folk were taking their mums out to lunch, and spoiled their day. I was going crazy with emotion, and my best friend was hurting. Asked to leave, we toured other venues, driving on the wrong side of the road until, hardly seeing what I was doing, I nearly knocked down a mother and baby on a pedestrian crossing before finally screeching to a halt at the York Bar Working Men's Club (WMC), where I went on a complete rampage during which I had a glass smashed over my head. With blood pouring from the wound, I smashed the windows with a bin, knocked out a committee man, and flung a chair at other men – unfortunately it missed the target and struck a lady. Someone else hit me with a hammer, and, when I came round in the police cells, all I could remember was being hit with the hammer – I was always justifying my actions.

But it was to prove another major turning point in my life. I was charged with seven offences and was evidently going back to prison. It was all over the internet and the papers. I started to panic. I was in the middle of a big building contract and I was looking after my daughter at weekends.

Then I had this weird conversation with Cliff, who was talking about "conscience" and playing with a knife. He was wracked with guilt and shame over his escapades with prostitutes and orgies and so on. He was doing strange things, such as paying in advance for his daughter's birthday party, and I later recognized in retrospect that he was tying up loose ends.

If Mother's Day was bad, Father's Day (three months later) was far worse. Cliff was supposed to have come round to pick up some radiators, but never turned up. When he didn't answer his phone, I walked down to his house with Alice on my shoulders. I knocked on the door and threw pebbles up at the window, but there was no answer.

I got a friend to take Alice off to my sister's, and other friends came round as we started to worry. I kicked in the panel of the front door. The house was immaculately clean, but there was blood on the bathroom door, drops of blood along the floor, and smears on the bedroom door. There were more bloodstains on a pile of money and on the bedroom wall, so we figured (or rather hoped) he might have taken himself off to hospital. But then the terrible reality hit us. Cliff was sitting down behind an alcove covered an inch-thick in blood and immersed in his own faeces and urine. It was a dreadful, shocking sight I would not wish on my worst enemy. And he was my best friend! He was sitting in a ju-jitsu fighting position with his legs crossed in the same clothes I had seen him wearing three days earlier. There was a knife in his right hand and a gaping hole in his neck. One of my friends tried to resuscitate him, but it was obviously no good as he had clearly been dead for some time. It was 15 June, the same day that young Carl had been killed back in 1992. I didn't want to go anywhere near the body and had a flashback of finding my mum lying dead on the sofa – something I had never dealt with, and which had destroyed my life and fuelled my rage and insecurity.

I got on the phone, ringing everybody, and in no time the house was flooded with people, including the police, of course. I was on autopilot with shock and immediately went on a non-stop seventy-two-hour bender in a bid to avoid facing reality. I also felt duty-bound to unravel the mess left by his sudden death, like rents that needed paying and bills that required sending out, all the while trying to make some sense of Cliff's wasted life. I felt I had lost my right arm, and knew that if I didn't change my ways I could end up in the same predicament.

The police tried to prevent us having a wake because of the form of many of those who would turn up at the funeral, which included Hell's Angels and heavy-duty career criminals. But there was no trouble, and when the cops knocked on my door next morning, it wasn't to arrest me this time; it was to thank me for keeping the peace! The pall-bearers, which included me, were probably too tired to cause any mayhem as they had carried the coffin for at least a mile to the church, and Cliff was no lightweight.

A 31 July 2008 report in *The Star*, reporting on my Doncaster Crown Court appearance for the pub rampage, said I had gone berserk after being banned from the York Bar WMC in Cusworth, taking on most of the committee members before I was overpowered. I injured several people at the club, and at one stage tore up fencing and threw chairs at members after drinking too much. The judge spared me jail after he heard that I was battling both the booze and my explosive temper by having psychotherapy, and had also saved the building business of a friend who had committed suicide so his widow and children would not be reduced to poverty. Recorder Jeremy Barnett told me: "I am satisfied, having read detailed reports, that you do have a condition which is capable of being treated, and it *is* being treated, and for that reason I am prepared to give you a chance. I take the view that you are doing your best to lay to rest these demons."

He imposed a twenty-six-week jail sentence, suspended for eighteen months, and a community order which included an anger management and alcohol treatment programme. I was also ordered to pay £175 compensation to the club and £200 to the female member who was hit by a chair. I admitted assault, affray, criminal damage, and driving while over the alcohol limit, for which I was banned from driving for two years.

I decided things had to change and willingly submitted to treatment for anger management and alcohol abuse through what is known as Cognitive Behavioural Therapy.

Bereavement counselling was now added to my list of treatments, but at the same time I slipped into more drinking despite efforts to stop me. I even started going to spiritualist venues trying to communicate with Cliff through mediums, tarot cards, and the occult. I was still searching for my identity, asking "Who am I?"; I guess this was part of my ongoing search. I got involved with a spirit medium after bumping into her while watching a cage fight. I became sucked into this world in subtle ways, such as having my mum described to me by someone who didn't know her; it was the enemy, Satan, at work again, though I didn't know it at the time. Just as I was getting my head together, having come out of serious drug pushing, to which I never returned, I was falling into another devilish trap. I dabbled with crystal balls and attended psychic fairs. I thought I was in church!

I subsequently joined a friend for a holiday in Cyprus where, by a sunny poolside, I was able to process all that had transpired and start to seriously question where life was taking me. I might otherwise have been tipped over the edge. Everything stopped. I saw that there was another way to live, and I actually felt half-excited about going home and starting the process of change.

An amusing aspect of the anger-management course – not so much for the victim, though – was that I laid a guy out in the street during a lunch break, then went straight back to the class. He owed me money, and I suppose it only served to emphasize my need for the treatment.

Meanwhile, the case involving my Mother's Day rampage was taking a series of twists and turns. A legal argument arose over the proposed showing of CCTV footage of the incident as the assaults on me had been edited, and, through Freemasonry contacts, I learnt that I was to get four years; that it had all been "fixed" among the "brothers" of the secret society, some of whom I had obviously offended during what was billed by the prosecution as my "psychopathic rampage". In order to deal with this, I hired a solicitor who specialized in finding legal loopholes and, when the Crown Court hearing came up, a seething judge found his hands were tied and was forced to send the case back to Doncaster Magistrates. As a result I was now also involved in a separate civil case about the legality of the trial. It had been a tactic of mine to delay sentencing – I had learnt how to manipulate the system – but it was also because I discovered that the Freemasons had stitched me up. At the same time I got into a dispute over access to Alice, which would involve a separate appearance in court.

Around this time I flew to Egypt on a pilgrimage to Mount Sinai as part of another spiritual quest influenced by my voracious appetite for reading while inside. I just felt I needed to find myself. Once there, I was accompanied up the mountain by a group of Muslims. They were also on pilgrimage on their way to Mecca. The ascent was not a pleasant experience for me because I was suddenly inflicted by terrible stomach cramps followed by a violent bout of sickness and diarrhoea. I phoned my spirit medium, only to be told it was all the bad coming out of me, to be replaced by goodness. There was a church and a mosque on the mountaintop, but the church was locked, which didn't impress me. However, I was inspired by the heavenly singing of a group of Chinese. I could tell they were using the word "Hallelujah" and started crying my eyes out with the beauty of the song. It was a mountaintop experience I could never forget, standing in the place where Moses had stood thousands of years earlier. It was very special. But I was nevertheless greatly relieved to get back to my hotel room where I collapsed for forty-eight hours with severe food poisoning which necessitated an operation on my return.

Although the criminal case was working in my favour, legal access to Alice was being blocked. It was January 2009 and I was told to reapply after another twelve months, but I wouldn't see her again for three years! Though no longer on the hard stuff, I was still smoking "wacky baccy", some of which accompanied me in the crevices of my bottom on a holiday flight to Bulgaria, where I was to meet up with friends. Having boarded the plane after an all-night binge, I naturally soon fell asleep and woke up busting for the toilet. Without thinking, I flushed my precious weed into the rare atmosphere five miles above the earth. As a chronic smoker, I didn't know how I was going to survive a fortnight without it. In fact, it made me hyperactive and I became "Mr Party", exhausting everyone else as I kept going like a Duracell bunny. Then I met a young lady I felt I had "seen" in a vision during a hypnotherapy session as part of my dabbling with spiritualism – dark-haired, olive-skinned, and Mediterranean. Her name was Lenka, and I spent a week romancing her in an idyllic location by the sea.

Paradise was soon lost, however, when I returned to my old stomping ground. I was arrested and charged with threatening behaviour for trying to take the law into my own hands over a rape case involving a friend, and was back on remand in the late summer of 2010 for assaulting a girlfriend – not deliberately, as it happened. She was injured as a result of my kicking in her door. In addition, I was taken by surprise when I discovered that the plumber among our building subcontractors also turned out to be a police special. In a state of paranoia over what he might know about my illicit activities, I resorted to threatening and intimidating behaviour towards him and was sent to Hull prison (Doncaster wouldn't take me as I knew too much about the system there). I spent three months at Hull, during which time I attended chapel once again. In December 2010 I was sentenced to eight months, which I had already served either on remand or curfew, which meant being "tagged" by wearing a chip on my ankle so the police were able to detect my whereabouts at all times. The rest was suspended, so the punishment amounted to little more than a slap on the wrist.

Chapter 15

DIVINE APPOINTMENT

Doing time in Hull was tough. It was about twenty weeks, and I was starting to struggle through my sentences now. I felt alone, but I didn't want to be around others. The novelty of all the scams, schemes, and shenanigans we used to dream up had worn off and, in any case, there were hardly any "criminals" any more as virtually everyone was on heroin substitutes. By this time EU laws had made it illegal for prisons to insist on inmates detoxing because it denies their human rights! I'm told prisons now spend £4 million a year on methadone.

It was as orderly of the resettlement unit – designed to help prepare inmates for the world outside – that I became aware of the amount of money thrown at this, which simply creates a revolving-door scenario and never deals with the underlying issues and causes of the behaviour. It was because I knew the system inside out that I got this job, which dealt with things like housing benefits for which inmates could qualify on release. It was really a matter of local authorities delegating their services to me. I morphed into a member of staff because I felt so different from the other prisoners. I even did a mentoring course known as SOVA (Supporting Others through Voluntary Action) and, when I got out, signed up to learn more about this at Doncaster College. Meanwhile ,my new spirit medium acquaintances were "praying" for me – even casting spells in an effort to help me. I genuinely believe they were doing it with the best of intentions, searching for answers as I was doing, but they had been fed a lie.

So, at the start of 2011 I was determined to turn my life around. I was a single man, and I'd had enough of crime, drugs, and chasing women. I wanted to find a wife and settle down, and also help other offenders. I continued as a volunteer with SOVA at their Doncaster office, providing information, advice, and guidance. I became a qualified counsellor and mentor, and was even helping sex offenders! I got the bit between my teeth and threw everything into this work – all my clients were ex-offenders, most of whom I knew. I was eventually nominated for a paid post and my overseer at the time wrote a case study on me.

Then, on Valentine's Day, I met Carrie, a single mum. We had been communicating for a while over the internet, and, like Lenka in Bulgaria with whom I was still in touch, she ticked all the boxes I had been given in that spiritualist reading of "a dark-haired Mediterranean woman". She claimed to be half-Italian and a trainee teacher, but it wasn't true. I tried to send flowers to the school but obviously couldn't locate it. I got carried away with the romantic side of things and fell hopelessly in love, certain that this was the one for whom I had been waiting all this time. I had been playing the field and not caring for years, and now a lifetime's worth of emotion and love was poured into what turned out to be a doomed relationship, and was to set me down a suicidal path. But it all started off like a firecracker, and we became inseparable.

I had absolutely nothing, materially speaking; I was a volunteer committed to a course. But Carrie and her two children had moved into my house by April and my work for SOVA turned into a full-time paid job for a probationary period of six months. Then I came into some money in a very dubious fashion, winning a £10,000 insurance payout for injuries supposedly sustained by tripping over a pothole when in fact they had already been inflicted in a bare-knuckle fight. I bought a car and fishing equipment along with new clothes and pets for the kids. Everything was going swimmingly between us and I became a father-figure to her children. I wasn't able to see mine, so it filled a void. I proposed and we got engaged. In the summer we flew to Tenerife for a beautiful family holiday.

But after we got back I had a kind of revelation at a spiritualist meeting. I came down with a banging headache and suddenly knew that it was all hocus-pocus; it just wasn't right. I came home, collected all my psychic paraphernalia, took them outside, and burnt them. Within a fortnight our relationship, built on such flimsy foundations, started to unravel. One night I was awakened by a buzzing under my pillow. It was Carrie's phone with a message from a guy through an online dating service. Scrolling down, I found hundreds of them. I felt betrayed yet again, and my love for her was knocked out in one mighty blow. However, I clung on to the idea of a family and continued living with her. But my heart wasn't in it.

I was made redundant from SOVA and, with reckless abandon, set up a fake fashion business through buying clothes from an old contact. I slipped back into old ways, such as smoking cannabis, as I tried to deal with the pain of betrayal. And I was about to experience hell on earth.

It all began when Carrie came in from a night out saying she was pregnant (she had taken her own test) but wanted to get rid of the baby! It also turned out that she had actually been out with another bloke, not her sister as she had claimed. Seething, I drove off to Denaby, some miles away, to unburden myself with my stepbrother and ended up ringing her and telling her to get out of the house. I'd had enough. But as she and her mother were still there when I got back, I proceeded to march them out of the house. I was loud, but not violent. Carrie slapped me around the face, but I didn't retaliate to the slap. I smashed her phone instead and drove off, saying: "You're dead to me!" Obviously, the latter remark was meant in the sense of cutting off our relationship.

But the police were alerted and I was subsequently locked in a cell on suspicion of a double assault, threatening to kill them, and of having stolen goods – they may have been fakes, but they were *not* stolen. Being known as a criminal gangster was one thing, but I now had "wife-beater" added to my credentials in the minds of those who knew me. My reputation had taken a dive, and it hurt me.

I was later released without charge when the accusations against me were withdrawn, but was then handed a letter from Social Services saying that, owing to the risk of emotional harm, I was denied further contact with Carrie's children until a full risk assessment was carried out. At the same time it appeared that Carrie was trying to get the landlord to sign the house over to her. Meantime she moved to a bungalow and booked into an abortion clinic.

For a time we lived as a family behind the back of Social Services. She had apparently changed her mind and now wanted to be with me and have my baby.

We had the first scan of Chris (not yet knowing he was a boy) on my birthday, 12 January 2012, and that really hit me. I was desperate for security – a two-way relationship with his mother rather than a battle.

Then a gangster approached me, offering me £1,000 for information that would enable him to find a witness in a case. It served the purpose of sucking me deeper into the pit of drinking, partying, and general skulduggery that I had been hoping to leave behind. Soon enough I managed to get involved in a fracas outside my house and was duly charged with assaulting a police officer and growing cannabis. When released on bail, I knew I had blown it. My hand was smashed by a police baton and I was in excruciating pain and immediately admitted to hospital. The very last text I read before being put to sleep for the operation was from Carrie ending the relationship. She was six months pregnant and it was 21 April.

I signed myself out while still under anaesthetic, bandaged and with pins sticking out and munching pain-killers like sweets. I turned up at Carrie's in a complete mess, with blood leaking from the wound, and woke up in a police cell. I can remember punching the window (with my healthy hand) and storming off. I apparently then collapsed in the street. But it was alleged that I had three times smashed her head against either the kitchen wall or work surface and I was arrested for serious assault – yet she had no injuries! I pleaded not guilty on the advice of my solicitor, but I was wracked with guilt and the rumour mill was going crazy. However, I felt so ill I couldn't even stand up. I didn't even know whether I had done it or not; that's what scared me. The solicitor assured me that she would have been in intensive care if her claims were correct.

So I got remanded back to Doncaster Marsh Gate pending trial. My hand became infected, so I was returned to hospital where it was reset and I had the pins removed.

Back in prison, I rang my big sister Rosemary, only to be told: "It's all over the village. I don't want anything to do with you now." It was a terrible shock, but I can hardly blame her. My sisters had been a constant throughout my criminal career, standing by me through thick and thin. I had put them through hell, and they had been spat at, threatened, and abused on account of me. Now, in their minds, I had reached the depths of depravity with this alleged attack on the mother of my child. "I'm ashamed of you," Rosemary finished, and put the phone down. That was the final straw. I broke down crying and rang my solicitor asking how quickly he could get me in court. I wanted to plead guilty and get it all sorted out. I was desperate.

I was sentenced within days to forty-two weeks in prison – later reduced on appeal to twenty weeks – as well as being served with a restraining order on Carrie.

Shortly after starting my sentence, I was busy cleaning on the wing when I noticed these two guys. I thought they were CID men as they were wearing suits and carried a certain authority about them. So I casually wandered over in my shorts, flip-flops, and bare torso. This black man put his hand out and introduced himself: "Hi, I'm Bruce, and this is Ronan." It was Bruce Dyer, a famous footballer – the first teenager to be signed for £1 million. Bruce is founder of Love Life UK, an organization dedicated to sharing the gospel in prisons while offering help and support as well as playing five-a-side football.

He gave me a green card embossed with a picture of praying hands and invited me to join them in the chapel where they held meetings on Tuesdays and Thursdays. I started to go along, and we talked about the Bible and shared our life experiences. I began to read the Bible, but didn't feel worthy to be part of that world. I thought I'd be burned at the stake if I walked into a church.

I was released in early July and Chris was born three weeks later. I heard that Carrie wanted me back and that one of the police officers from the case had been hassling her for a date. So we were reconciled, making a fresh start in spite of orders designed to protect her from domestic violence at my hands, and we more or less lived together for the next few months. I sneaked into the house through the side door, and bonded with my son as I fed and changed him. I started a money-making operation turning red diesel into white through the use of filters. I saw Alice for the first time in three years, and Emily was also now part of my life. (She had contacted me via social media around the time of her twelfth birthday, and we had slowly begun to communicate.)

With my 2013 birthday approaching, Rosemary (now reconciled with me) was arranging a party involving all my children together for the first time. Unfortunately Carrie and I were by this time at loggerheads once more, and it coincided with a report from a new social worker that I had been seen with her. I subsequently told her a few home truths – that she was a liar and a schemer –

which evidently wasn't too well received as I woke up with an Alsatian barking beside my bed and a house full of police. I was arrested for breach of a restraining order and taken to Doncaster police station where I heard that I was being accused of turning up at Carrie's house after not seeing her for nine months, slapping her, and taking the child hostage.

Remanded in custody, I walked back into Marsh Gate prison on 4 January and the next day completely broke down when attending a group Bible meeting led by Bruce and Ronan. The severity of the whole situation hit me like a ton of bricks when I returned to the wing. For all my tough-guy persona, I was scared stiff of losing everything once more and facing another battle of having to rebuild my shattered life. I had built a bond with my son, I had my daughters back, and now I was looking at another long sentence for something I had certainly not done. It seemed that I had lost all meaning and purpose in life. I was distraught, lost, ashamed, and broken as a man. My reputation was in tatters and my family had had enough. My children were once again fatherless. I had survived heroin, living on the streets of London, and six prison sentences, but this time I was truly at rock bottom. I couldn't see a way out and felt totally defeated. I knew for certain I just couldn't cope with another sentence; I was mentally and emotionally destroyed, and had nothing left.

Lost in a sea of utter despair and hopelessness, I decided to end my life. I knew I couldn't hang myself, as the prison is virtually suicide proof. I couldn't cut myself either because of the horror of what I had witnessed with Cliff's death. So I decided to overdose. Since I had been put on a detox wing out of fears for the safety of other prisoners, I would have access to enough drugs to blow myself to smithereens.

All that changed after I had an awesome experience in the room where the Bible study was being held. There was a group of us with Bruce and Ronan and we got talking on the topic of fathers. Each one of us was not seeing his children and hurting as a result. In my case I had just missed the chance of seeing my three kids together for the first time. There was a real brokenness in that gathering of men. We all felt we'd let our children down, that we were failures as men and as fathers, and some of us were fatherless ourselves. Ronan was a widower at the time, though he has since remarried. There were lots of tears, emotions, and shame. We all held hands and stood in a circle, praying for the restoration of families. We prayed for fathers – to become better fathers and good role models, for our own fathers, and for our hurts – and the presence of God dropped into that room in an amazing way; the atmosphere was tangible. I genuinely believe God came into that room and answered our prayers that day, even if we have yet to see the manifestation of it.

Something inside me was transformed. I left the room totally ashamed and convicted of my failures as a man, as a father, and as a partner – in truth, the presence of God had convicted me deeply.

As I was leaving the meeting, I was given a "goodie bag", which included a notepad, a pencil, a chocolate bar, and a book – Joyce Meyer's *Battlefield of the Mind*.

I returned to my cell and, as soon as the door was shut, dropped to my knees a broken man. Having nowhere else to turn, I cried out to God: "If you are there and you're hearing my prayers, put a white dove outside my cell window. Show me that you are with me." I had been watching the pigeons gathering daily on a ledge outside, desperately looking for a sign of hope, that someone was there to help me.

I went to sleep and, when I awoke next morning, lit a roll-up and looked to see a flock of pigeons waiting on the ledge outside as usual. Then they spread their wings and lifted off in what seemed like slow motion, just as a white dove came in to land in their place. It was the sign I needed, and I now knew Jesus was with me. I dropped to my knees again; at that moment I gave my life to Jesus Christ and became a born-again Christian. It was 17 January 2013.

I had no idea at the time that the dove was a symbol of the Holy Spirit, who is said to have descended "like a dove" on Jesus at his baptism. But I needed that confirmation; I had been searching for so long – I had been lied to, betrayed, and abused, and couldn't face any more hurt. I needed to know. God honoured that cry, sending a sign to say: "Son, it's time to come home."

Chapter 16

FREE AT LAST!

As I got up from that life-changing prayer, I had this big surge of emotion. I was so elated I went running down the stairs shouting, "There is a God; there is a God!" I think everyone reckoned I had gone off my rocker. Then, almost immediately, before I even had time to gather my thoughts, an officer came to me, saying, "Pack your stuff; you're going to Leeds on a security move." I usually would have kicked off in response to that sort of thing by doing something crazy like sticking a razor blade in my mouth. But something inside stopped me, and I reacted with uncharacteristic calmness. I packed all my stuff, said my goodbyes, and was on the bus within an hour. Now I know it was just as well. Doncaster wasn't the ideal place for me to shed my old skin, as it were, because it was all too familiar. I needed to be sent into my own personal wilderness. Don't forget – I was still emotionally very tender; I had been on the verge of committing suicide only the night before. It had all happened so fast. So I was full of apprehension with a slight twist of excitement as I was being driven to Leeds. I was trying to figure out some logic to it all, but all I knew was that God was real.

As we approached the forbidding sight of Armley jail in Leeds, my heart suddenly sank as I felt lost and not sure what to expect. It helped when I arrived that all my cellmates on the induction wing were somehow linked to God – one was a Roman Catholic and another had just started asking the big questions about life. I had brought the "goodie bag" of Christian literature I had been given in Doncaster and began reading Joyce Meyer's *Battlefield of the Mind*. She had a history of abuse and explained how we can give all the pain of our memories to Jesus. I developed an intense thirst for reading this book and looking up every Scripture reference in the prison Bible while also making notes with the pad and pen I had been given.

One of the first things I did was write a letter addressed to everyone I had hurt (just as an exercise in helping to deal with my past), setting fire to it afterwards. It was like peeling off the first layer of the onion skin. Then, metaphorically speaking, I put all the rage and anxiety I had built up over the previous twenty years – what Joyce Meyer refers to as "stinking thinking" – at the cross where Jesus took my sins upon himself. I envisaged all my anger and garbage as a ball which I placed at Jesus' feet, and, when I woke up next morning, something inside me had changed forever. I was simply bathed in perfect peace, and I knew it was supernatural. All the rage, unpredictability, violence, and hatred that had churned around in my stomach like clothes in a washing machine for years had vanished overnight, and it was as if I had a waterfall of love pouring out of me. I remember standing on the second-floor landing leaning over the metal railing surrounded by manic activity, and yet for me it was all in slow motion. Amid the storm of everything going on around me, I was at peace with myself, with the world, and with God. Even as I looked up at the window of my cell, all I could see was a cross, shaped by a combination of light and beams. As I knelt down, looking up at the sky, tears streamed down my face. I knew I had found "the way, the truth and the life", as Jesus described himself. I knew he was close to me; I could feel it in my heart.

My priorities had changed. I was now sensitive to the burdens and troubles of other people. I developed a voracious appetite for Christian literature, reading book after book. There was *Once an Addict*, by Barry Woodward, and *Hell's Angel*, the story of Brian Greenaway, a former Hell's Angel who also found Christ while doing time in prison. But I was still naïve and unaware of the danger of certain types of spiritualist activity, such as dabbling with mediums, witchcraft, and the occult as I had been doing. Claire, the prison chaplain, put me right about that and also prayed against the evil influence these activities had left in my spirit, at which point I felt as if a black cloud had lifted off me. Later that night my hands glowed hot as I had an experience of the Holy Spirit coming near.

After that, I just wanted to be down at the chapel all the time. When the Wednesday night Christian team came along, they laughed when they saw how I was trying to pull the jail doors down in my eagerness to attend. I was so full of the joy of the Lord, so boisterous I was literally bouncing around wanting to tell everyone what had happened to me. The team were from the Abundant Life Church in Bradford and, in the chapel, I sat next to a lady called Anne-Marie. They were giving out the very same goodie bags I had received in Doncaster, and when I told them how I had already received one there, Anne-Marie explained that she was the one who had actually packed them for Doncaster! I was amazed. Surely God was working at tying up all the loose ends, weaving things together in such a perfect pattern. It was another symbol of the divine dove bringing transformation to my life, now beginning its dramatic journey from that volatile young man with a violent streak and all that nastiness and replacing it with his love.

At the same time, however, I was still struggling with the accusations against me that had landed me behind bars for the seventh time. I was in a high-security prison on remand, accused of causing a hostage situation, and learnt that I had been refused bail. That would normally have set me off on a rampage, smashing things up, but I was perfectly calm and even tried to help others on the wing with their problems. I had surely deserved such punishment in the past, but there was clearly no justice involved this time. I then heard the distressing news that my son Chris had been taken out of Doncaster with his siblings and immediately asked to speak to Claire, the prison chaplain. She found me crying my eyes out over it all, and prayed that the truth would come out in my case.

The very next morning my cell door opened with the words: "Come on, you're going to Doncaster Court. Pack your stuff; you're not coming back here." I wasn't due in court for another week, so I wondered what was going on. I'd been in Leeds just a fortnight after three weeks in Doncaster's Marsh Gate prison – five weeks during which I had been on a 1,000-mile journey emotionally and spiritually.

I duly signed out and was soon on the bus back to South Yorkshire – a trip of some 30 miles. At Doncaster I was ushered into a holding cell where my solicitor arrived, beaming from ear to ear. "It's over!" he announced. Armed with the evidence we had presented, the prosecution had re-interviewed Carrie, who subsequently withdrew her statement and apologized for lying. It had all been a complete fabrication and the case against me had been dropped. "We just need to tidy up your order," he added, referring to my ban from living with her or seeing her children; it turned out she had been removed from Doncaster in case of any reprisals over the stitch-up. In the end I was given a two-week sentence for breaching this order, which of course I had already more than served. So I was released from Doncaster Magistrates as a free man with no other charges pending.

I bounced up the court stairs with my bin-liner of belongings and my Bible, with a zealous passion to share my new-found faith. I went straight to the pub where I quaffed a few pints and tried to tell everyone about Jesus. I didn't yet know any other way. Going for a drink was like putting on a comfortable pair of slippers. Though I had now started a new life, it came with heavy baggage from the old one I had followed for so long, and it would take time to let go of some habits. I was still shell-shocked by all that had happened, but I did feel different. Of course I was telling everyone about God and I suppose they thought I had gone crazy. Everyone was familiar with me flying into a rage with my unpredictable behaviour, and now I wanted to cuddle them! It would take some adjustments for friends and family to get their heads around the new me.

This was Friday 15 February 2013, and I knew for certain that I needed to get to church on the Sunday. Bruce Dyer, who had been the key influence in my conversion, was connected with Bentley Baptist Church.

When Sunday came around I woke up with a hangover. And so, full of apprehension and self-doubt, I went to church, feeling more than a little unworthy and with a bag of weed in my pocket. I was in a building full of people I had never met, but with a fearsome reputation in the area. Rough and ready as I was, however, I was just knocked back by the love I felt when I entered that building for the first time on 17 February 2013. I walked all the way up the aisle and sat on the front row. My arrival was also the answer to the church's corporate prayer. Only the week before Bruce had preached specifically about Jesus setting the prisoners free.

Then we started to sing. It wasn't like the hymns we had sung at school. The worship was led by a live band, and tears started streaming down my face. I threw my hands in the air and I knew I was free from all those years of pain, all that anger, jealousy, and strife, because I had been touched by Jesus Christ in prison. I cried like a baby, shedding tears of repentance, feeling dirty, ashamed, downtrodden. Tears became unspoken words washing out all the filth from the depths of my stomach-wrenching years of burdens, abuse, and betrayal. Although my mistakes were all forgotten and forgiven by Jesus, I didn't yet know how to let them go. I cried all the way through the worship.

Back at Leeds, the Wednesday before I went to court, Claire had brought me a "word" from Psalm 46 that she felt God had given her especially for me: "Be still, and know that I am God". The following Sunday, Julie Harrop, who turned out to be a former special constable, got up to preach. Her text was: "Be still, and know that I am God"! I was completely taken aback. I had never heard anyone preach like this before, and I wondered if this was some sort of conspiracy between church and Armley. How on earth did she know that Claire had given me that exact word just a week or so earlier in my prison cell?

My journey of self-discovery had begun, and all these "God-incidences" were further confirmation that I was in the right place. Now I had to start learning to live a new life that had begun at the cross of Christ, which I had discovered on my knees in prison.

Chapter 17

A NEW WAY OF LIVING

So I set off on a one-man crusade to change the world, with plenty of zeal but precious little wisdom. My personality tends to run ahead of myself, and the lack of discipline, structure, and patience was going to have to be tamed. I threw myself into whatever activity was put on by the church. If there was a prayer meeting or Bible study, I would attend it. I couldn't get enough of it. Had I not done so, I would never have made it.

I am so grateful for the serious discipleship programme laid on by Bentley Baptist Church to ensure that new converts get all the help they need. Undoubtedly, someone from my kind of background needed all the help he could get. I had to break free from twenty-plus years of living in a way that was almost completely opposite to the way a Christian should live. I had lived in a dark world, but had now come into the light. Humans are not robots; they can only pick up new habits gradually and with consistent, practical application. It wasn't going to be easy, and it certainly hasn't been so far. But this is where mentorship became so vital. Bruce counselled me to aim for "whiter than white" and Peter, the retiring pastor, for "no compromise". They started me on the process of straightening out my life. I was bubbling with joy but still following my old ways to a great extent. For example, I found myself praying at the bar for a man who had been diagnosed with terminal cancer, and when I had finished I bought him a pint so we could get drunk together. But there was a nagging inside me that somehow this way of life wasn't quite right. I was starting to think differently. Then one night I got drunk and woke up in the back seat of a car with no shoes or socks, and no clue as to how I got there. It was a frightening experience, so I decided that day to stop drinking. I have only had a handful of drinks since. It soon dawned on me that I should also give up smoking weed, though conquering the craving for cigarettes would take longer.

I was now going to church and attending prayer meetings, but I was still a mixed-up person. After all, my whole life up to that point had revolved around drink, drugs, and women. I wanted to share my experience with everyone I met. I'd walk into town asking people if I could pray for them and sharing what had happened to me. In my initial enthusiasm, I got involved in three different churches, including the Bradford fellowship that had been so helpful to me while I was at Leeds. Obviously that was too far away for the long term (about 40 miles), and I felt the need to get established at a specific home church where I knew I'd be looked after. But it was strategically placed key men of God who enabled me to build a solid foundation on Christ, and it was at Bentley that I was wonderfully mentored, guided, and transformed. It was also a huge help that this particular church was involved in sports outreach, which of course suited me perfectly with my rugby background. The retiring pastor, Peter Amos, had been chaplain of Barnsley FC for a number of years (and still is at the time of writing), while Dave Miller (one of the elders) was chaplain at my old Rugby League club, Doncaster Dons – how neat is that? And Barry Miller (no relation, but also an elder) was chaplain at Doncaster Rovers, where he had also once been captain! And of course there was Bruce, who had played at a high level all over the country.

For those who don't know, Bruce's talent as a striker was such that he became the first teenager in England to be signed for more than £1 million – £1.25 million to be exact – when he moved from Watford to Crystal Palace in 1994. In a senior career spanning fifteen years, he scored 119 goals – half of them (fifty-nine) during his five years and 181 appearances for Barnsley. He also played for Stoke City, Millwall, Sheffield United, Doncaster Rovers, Bradford City, Rotherham United, Chesterfield, and York City. And he represented England at U21 level but, despite scoring four goals in eleven games, was never capped at full level, though he did play a friendly for Montserrat against Ashford Town in 2007. Of course it was through his prison outreach ministry, Love Life UK, which he shares with his gospel-singer wife Janine, that I met him. The sporting connection was just a bonus.

Bruce has invested many hours of phone calls, emails, and texts in me. He's been a rock through the good, the bad, and the ugly, constantly reassuring and encouraging me and, most importantly, praying for and with me. The vital necessity of building on a biblical foundation, with a strong prayer life, along with accountability and a willingness to change, were all instilled in me. It's also worth pointing out, in view of my racist attitudes (more than partly built up by childhood abuse at the hands of a black woman), that Bruce is actually black! And through the link with him I have since shared my story with many different black churches. In fact, 90 per cent of the places I have visited outside my own church have been home to either Pentecostal or black African congregations. It's one of many examples of how God has turned something bad for good. Once I had found Jesus, I just wanted to give everyone what Bruce called the "Langham hug". I have since learnt a lot about black culture and now love Jamaican food, especially jerk chicken.

Also in constant communication with me was Dave Miller, who took on a father role in the many different aspects of rebuilding a shattered life. Then there was another David, a semi-retired teacher, who taught me about money management, creating a spreadsheet and budgeting plan as we started wading through the £20,000-plus mountain of debt I had accumulated through my wayward living. I learnt about values and integrity, and I couldn't have got through the early days without these beautiful people.

* * *

It's worth mentioning how I dealt with that debt, as an example of God's provision. At first, I just buried my head in the sand. My attitude was that anything pre-me becoming a Christian didn't matter – I am a new creation, and all that. But at heart I wanted to honour that debt, and the senior leaders at church were all in agreement that I should.

I got advice from National Debtline, a very good free government service, and Christians Against Poverty, and StepChange. Everybody took one look and recommended I go bankrupt. I didn't want to do that because I still remembered the times when bankrupts went into the papers and everyone could relish the scandal – and I didn't think it was what God wanted. "This man is saved, hallelujah! And he's taken us for more than a grand" – that wouldn't be a convincing witness.

With David's help, I contacted every single creditor I had, and offered a payment plan of £1 a month. I also asked for settlement figures. Then, in reverse order, from the smallest to the largest settlement figure, I started to work through and pay them off.

As I began to understand how the world's money system works I realized I could use finance and capital in a way that benefits. My bank advised me that I could get a high-interest loan, which would clear my county court judgment, which would reset my credit file, which would then let me get a low-interest loan to pay off that high-interest loan. That way, I was using credit wisely.

I also asked other men at Bible study to pray with me about my debt. As a result, I've had debts like £1,700 settle at a hundred-and-something pounds, and I've had debts just disappear completely. Later, as my business grew and more income came in, the more I could pay off. But it wasn't the straight answer to my financial problems, because I immediately decided to use the money saved for the kingdom. Impulsively and foolishly, I went straight off and sponsored five kids, which wasn't sustainable. It's better to offer a little at a time, sustainably.

This was also when I stopped smoking. I'd titled one column in the spreadsheet "Lungs", showing my cigarette expenditure. It was something like £200 a month and I had a shortfall of about £150 a month on my total outgoings. It was apparent I couldn't afford to smoke. I had tried several times in my own strength to stop, but it always lasted just a few hours. I prayed about it with David.

That night I went to a prayer service, and the preacher pointed out that when the collection plate comes round, we usually think it's a financial thing – but there may be times when God wants other offerings. I didn't have any money on me, so I screwed up my pack of cigs and put it into the offering plate. Market value, about £7. I offered up my smoking to God to do with as he wished. The power of God came over me and I went to the floor, out cold – not the first time I'd had that experience, but the first from the Lord. After that, I stopped smoking.

I didn't know at the time that I had a spirit of poverty within me – more on that later. The biggest challenge was overcoming a poverty mindset. My revelation came when I didn't have a washing-up bowl. I was collecting something for a family appeal, so I also asked the lass, "Do you mind if I have a washing-up bowl? I haven't got one."

She said, "Yes, of course you can."

When I turned it over, I saw the price label on it. It was £1. She'd got it from the pound shop. I realized that I'd gone without something, for months, that I could have had for £1.

That is the mindset I had to change. It's counter-intuitive, but I now deliberately go to more affluent gyms, eat in better restaurants. I can end up spending ten pounds to save one. If I were to go abroad and get a cheap hotel, then pay for aircon, Wi-Fi, food, and add it all up, I may pay more than I would have if I'd gone to a five-star all-inclusive.

At the same time, I've got to be careful because there is a lot of misguided teaching about prosperity: "If you give, you're going to get a blessing." People give, just to get bailed out of their own troubles. But God is our

Father, and, as the Scriptures say, if we can give our own children good gifts, imagine what he can give us.

* * *

Within just three weeks of the time when we prayed in Doncaster prison for the restoration of fathers and of families, my daughter Emily (by now a teenager) had moved in with me. Not long afterwards, Alice also began staying over at weekends. Emily was depressed and struggling with various issues at the time and her grandmother was dying of cancer. So I trust and hope that I managed to provide some stability for her. Apparently she had made an overnight decision to come and live with me, and her mum dropped her off. It was the start of restoration in our family, and those prayers offered inside prison walls were already beginning to be answered. But we had no relationship; we had to start from scratch and it was a big thing for both of us. I was wracked with guilt for having not been a proper father to her. I felt the need to tell her everything. So, night after night we talked in an effort to build some foundations. I also had no job or income yet. The church was buying me food and individual members were privately helping me out with bills. A lovely couple, Diane and Jim Clifton, decorated Emily's bedroom.

Everything I had earned in the past had been done illegally. My house had effectively been a cannabis farm before, with a secret room where I grew the stuff. (It's still there, but now it's a broom closet.) Now all that had been stripped out. I also took up a parenting course and prayed for a job. There was a presentation at The Dome, a big leisure centre in town, by an organization called Herbalife, seeking representatives to spread their message offering advice on nutrition and diet. I didn't think much of it at first, but was impressed by one speaker who said that if you focused on looking after customers' best interests, the money you made would be just a by-product. That spoke volumes to me, so I decided to take a leap of faith by using up virtually all the money we had for shopping that week (with Emily's permission) in order to join. And the next day my sister turned up with a week's worth of shopping! I set about the task of building up my Herbalife opportunity by helping people to improve their health and well-being.

Meanwhile, I travelled all over the place sharing my testimony; my new life was a whirlwind. Anne-Marie, the lady from Bradford I'd met in Leeds prison, sent me a ticket for a big conference and, in an auditorium full of people, I somehow found myself sitting next to her. She handed me a note about a baptism service they were holding on 21 April.

That date! It was the birthday of my childhood friend Rob; and, the year before, 21 April 2012 had seen the arrest which set off a series of shameful, dreadful episodes. Now I was handed a leaflet all about a new beginning. I already wanted to be baptized – like any new convert, I felt dirty, shamed, and I wanted to be cleansed. I had asked about it at Bentley, but when I saw it was available in Bradford on that date, that settled it.

Emily came with me. The morning of the baptism I got up with such joy in my heart and such excited nerves. For the journey over to Bradford, every single traffic light was green. I was one of ninety-six new Christians immersed in a pool in front of hundreds of others, signifying our death (full immersion under the water) and resurrection to new life with Christ. I even picked up the pastor and spun him round when I came up out of the water. He tried to high-five me but I was so out of it as I jumped about and celebrated that I didn't notice, and he had to turn it into a pat on the back. I was so full of joy. It was a perfect day and the first significant step in my Christian journey. I felt symbolically clean.

My friends Graham and Catherine put on a full dinner and barbecue after the event. We had homeless people there eating with us, so the atmosphere was absolutely wonderful. They'd recorded my baptism and gave me a DVD of it as a special gift. Watching it was the first time I noticed the attempted high five.

The hardest thing about baptism is the first time you commit a sin after the event. You think that you're unclean again. The water is significant for cleansing, but then the baptism of the Spirit is a *continual* washing, and that is what gets you through the hard times, when everything you can think of is going wrong. That's the reality when evil forces are assigned against you. Anybody who wants to get into Christianity because they think it's just a good way of getting good luck or good fortune, then I'm sorry, it's probably not for you. Anyone who would choose Christianity as a way out is probably a little bit deluded.

There was still no particular structure to my life. Whatever was going on in church life, I was there. After all, I had lived in a state of absolute chaos for so long, lurching from one crisis to the next. I had to be reined in every now and then.

Someone said I needed to put my roots down, so I prayed about this, and, when I was sent a photograph of the Bentley church, with a note from a friend saying he felt prompted by the Lord to send it to me, I knew I had the answer. Meanwhile, I became embroiled in a court case in a bid to gain access to my son Chris, and my mentors were concerned that I was putting myself under too much pressure.

Life is a learning curve, and it is sometimes necessary to withdraw from certain company or situations if their influence isn't helpful. People I had known for years simply vanished out of my life, as I guess they couldn't cope with my new identity in Christ. The result was more stability in my life, and I decided simply to trust God with the whole issue of access to Chris.

From this time Dave Miller started to have real input in my life, along with Bruce, of course, and life began to take on much more structure. I was going through assessments to be officially allowed to have Emily with me. There were lots of appointments, as well as the parenting course and my work for Herbalife. I was truly happy. I'd walk around the local lake listening to worship music as well as sermons by Derek Prince. All I wanted to do was worship God and cuddle everyone. Yet as I hugged people, they cried and started to share their hearts with me. Many people started to ask questions as they began to see the transformation in my life. A close friend came to see me and immediately broke down. He came to church the following Sunday and I had the privilege of leading him to the cross. It was a beautiful moment, and the start of an incredible journey of purpose.

For much of the first few months of my new life I was basking in the glow of the dramatic change that had come over me. Like a newborn baby, I was somewhat protected from the harsh realities of what life as a Christian can still throw at you. I was in a bubble walking on water ,as it were. Just because you have started out on what Jesus refers to as "life in all its fullness" doesn't mean it's all going to be a bed of roses. In fact, in many cases the problems actually increase, as I was soon to find out, except that now I was at least living a life of purpose and truth. The Bible says, "Therefore, if anyone is in Christ, the new creation has come: The old has gone, the new is here!" (2 Corinthians 5:17).

So for a while I was cocooned in a kind of spiritual incubator, resting in the Father's love just as a newborn baby lies on its parent's chest. The Lord eases us into his world gently before letting us loose as soldiers of Christ. Eventually we find our feet as toddlers who, quite naturally, keep falling over as we learn to walk, and then, as we get stronger in our faith, we are sent into battle. For example, I now had a conscience and people began to rely on me for various things, and by the grace of God my life served as an example to others.

I soon realized that spiritual warfare is something that is going on all the time, that the enemy of our souls is always out to destroy our witness and drag us down, and we can only survive with the armour God gives us. So getting up early to pray and study the Word of God, along with various other Christian disciplines, became essential as I faced many challenging situations. It was a case of finding out how to live and repenting of actions that weren't right. Patience has always been a problem with me, but I have made progress in this area since becoming a Christian, although it's a lesson I haven't yet fully learned. Sometimes, when trials beset us, it's because there's something in us that needs to change. And yet the more we step out in faith and try to live a holy life, the more opposition we face. That comes with the territory.

Chapter 18

A NEW WORLD

God continued to work dramatically in my life. Income was now coming in, my budgeting was working, and there was something to get up for each day. I had found the answer that could also change the lives of other people. Life wasn't just about me any more. Emily was warded into my care and committed her life to the Lord at a youth event. In fact, lots of people came to Christ after I shared my story with them. Life needs to have a goal, and I knew that the purpose of all this transformation was that God was preparing me for a new life-path. I had tried everything the world had to offer, but now I realized that without Jesus, there's no point.

After learning about the spiritual power of prayer and fasting at a conference in London, I launched out on my first-ever three-day fast. I genuinely believe that we should have a discipline of fasting in our armoury – a day a week, a day a month, whatever it is that works for you. You've got to work that out with God. God knows your heart. In Matthew 17:21, Jesus identifies a type of spirit that can only come out "by prayer *and fasting*". If you've got issues over things like family, violence, and illness, then prayer and fasting really does make a difference. You feel closer to God. You hear a bit more clearly once you've got past the headaches and the detoxification and the irritability.

Fasting sounds easy to the uninitiated, if not especially attractive. You just cut down on eating, right? Wrong. Fasting is hard and takes practice. Scripture says God won't take you beyond what you can handle (1 Corinthians 10:13) – but with training, that point gets further away. As a personal trainer, I train people in fitness. Spiritual training works in the same way – over a period of time you find you can handle just that bit more and then that bit more again.

I don't, however, believe in things like social media fasts or going without TV – for me, fasting is going without food, for spiritual purposes. I also believe in following the biblical example. If you are praying for a particular need or things in general, I think a sustained period of partial fast is required. The big ones – forty days and nights with no food, and things like that – are for when you are waiting for a significant move from God. There have been times when I have been waiting for answers to prayer and have done a Daniel fast, which is a vegetarian fast, as in Daniel 1, for longer periods. The Esther fast – three days on just water, no food, as in Esther 4 – is for life and death matters. Esther risked death if she didn't get it right.

Now I fast a lot less than I used to, for two reasons. One is that I wasn't doing it right. I wasn't breaking my fast correctly. I was going from poor eating habits, to fasting, and back again to poor eating. My weight was up and down, and my digestive system suffered. In fact, you should break a fast gently, starting with small bits of food – maybe a bit of fruit – and build up gradually. But secondly – following some very informative experiences, which you'll read about later – I learned to let grace into my life without the fasting. Matthew 4 says Jesus went into the wilderness to fast, "led by the Spirit". I often fasted without clear instruction.

At the time, all this understanding lay ahead of me; my motivation was wrong. I read about the power of the Holy Spirit after Jesus had been in the wilderness, and I was craving miracles. I wanted to see people get out of wheelchairs. But no, that's not always God's way.

Still, at one point, it seemed that people were getting healed every single day. I went to the shop and the lady behind the counter had been crippled with a bad back for months, so I just prayed with her and it went. And then I found myself starting to look for it. Like someone once said, "To a man with a hammer, everything looks like a nail." Going through town, I'd want to stop and pray for everybody – but out of my need, rather than theirs. I had to learn that there might be one clear person that God wants to heal for a particular purpose, and after that you're taking on stuff that you shouldn't. In Acts 3, Peter and John healed a lame man who begged at the Temple every day. Well, if he really was there *every* day then Jesus must have encountered him too – and *not* healed him. It wasn't the time.

Although the discipline is designed to deepen our communication with God and thus build our faith, it also leaves us open to temptation – and not just for food! The truth is that the more we step out in God, the more the devil is on our back, as Jesus discovered during his forty days. So, after my first-ever fast of not eating for three days, I made the mistake of breaking my fast with a meal at the house of a young lady I had befriended, and we ended up in bed! That completely threw me, and I sensed an immediate stop in the flow of God's Spirit within me. I lost my sense of peace and felt I had betrayed the Lord. And it wasn't the only fling of a sexual nature that slowed me down during my initial few months as a Christian.

Living as a single Christian man was as different as chalk from cheese to the reckless, wayward life I had once lived. Yes, I had a new spirit in me. But I was still a man, with needs, desires, and longings. I was in a whole new world. How on earth was I to make the switch from having a girl in every port to being a married man who's never even been on a date because women were throwing themselves at me since I was a teenager? That was the big question I faced, and conversion in and of itself is not a quick and easy solution. The love of God flows into our lives immediately when we ask Jesus to come in, but character building is something we need to work on with God's help. He gives us the equipment – the Word of God and the Holy Spirit to guide and strengthen us – but we have to apply it and cover ourselves with it as with a soldier's armour. I was still a young recruit with a lot of mouth but little wisdom, and was being cut down by the enemy because I was going into battle ill-equipped in terms of character and moral strength. I didn't know the rules and commands, and they cover every aspect of life, including no sex outside marriage.

Trouble was, I was the most impulsive man you could ever meet and wasn't going to change overnight. For example, I got a bee in my bonnet about a certain young lady at church I thought the Lord was pointing out as my future wife. And I was foolish enough to approach her and deliver "the message", succeeding only in freaking her out.

Looking back now I can laugh about it, but at the time it was horrendous – for me and for her. It was my second or third time in church and I didn't understand about being given "words". I should have gone to somebody and asked how this worked – they'd have told me to take it to the Lord and wait until I'd got full clarity. Maybe if it had been done more diplomatically or tactfully, over a period of time, then it might have been received completely differently.

Thankfully, she and her father never held it against me. It could possibly have been a swerve ball to cause havoc in my life, because I was so hurt by the rejection – and already feeling unwelcome, because somehow the word had gone around, based on my old life, that I was a violent, nasty piece of work, a serial womanizer – that I nearly left the church. I was strongly tempted to head off for a church in Bradford. As it turned out, the mentor that they had lined up for me there is no longer a Christian, and the church there was full of young, single women. So for a guy who was fresh out of prison, with loads of young, attractive women and not a lot of accountability, that could have gone so, so wrong. Had I gone off in a huff, I'd have got sniped at Bradford, no two ways about it.

As a result of this and similar incidents, I was shunned by some in the church – and I take things very personally, even more so as a Christian. Whereas in the past I would have lashed out and dealt with it by means of brute force, now I just felt emotionally ripped to bits. I had to learn to toughen up and develop a thicker skin. Constant battles would ensue over issues affecting conscience, compromise, and character as I gradually learnt to seek guidance from the Lord as well as from mature Christians.

But, for all that, I was clearly a changed man. When I discovered an online pervert was trying to groom my daughter, I actually rang the police rather than settling the issue with my fists. Violence simply isn't in me any more; it's not being a grass to call the police when there's somebody grooming your daughter.

Once a particular bailiff came round for a small sum that had already been addressed. He just walked into the house and confronted the painter doing the decorating – I wasn't there. It got very heated and threatening, and the painter called me. Instead of going right round to sort it out, I told him to ring the police.

There was a time when I had a violence marker put against my name. Whenever my name appeared in a call, it said: "Known to be violent towards police; deploy pepper spray." They would have been round in minutes, not the hours it took them in this case.

But when I came back from work that night with my son in the car next to me, the head of police pulled up behind me. He let my son put his hat on and he said, "Listen, Allen, we've had lots of run-ins over the years with you, but you can come to us." And he shook my hand.

I was gradually being reprogrammed to live right, but it was difficult. I was still prone to feel rejection all too easily, and took it hard when Emily decided to return to her mum and granddad. Tough, emotional issues kept bombarding me, but at the same time I had never felt so close to God and so at peace. It's a journey of personal revelation as I continue to learn more about myself as well as God. And that journey has also run parallel to working on this book, raising issues that have constantly challenged me. Yet it continues to amaze me how much of a difference it has made to my life since I laid down my burdens at the cross of Christ.

Chapter 19

THE WIDOW'S MITE

Early in 2014 I was sponsored for an eight-week course in personal training at the David Lloyd Centre in Enfield, north-east London. I had sworn I would never return to London when I left the capital in a prison van, but now I was back there a new man. On a day off from college, I took the Tube into central London to revisit my old haunts, focusing on the Covent Garden and Leicester Square area where I used to hang out.

It was a hot day and virtually the first person I came across as I ventured out into the open air was a homeless man called Luke. It turned out he had been there for all of fifteen years, since the time I too was on these streets with all hope apparently lost. He had been a chef, but had taken to drink following the breakdown of a relationship, as a result of which he lost both his home and his job. I identified with him, shared my story and some scriptures, bought him a cup of coffee, and prayed for him.

Perversely, the police were ringing my phone as we were praying on that West End pavement! My daughter was having a party and they had just raided my house on suspicion of drugs being used. No one was arrested, but it seemed perfectly timed to put me off my stroke. Was this the enemy of God having a go?

Apart from that, my return visit to London was this time blessed from start to finish. While there I attended the Enfield Christian Revival Centre, having searched for a local "Spirit-filled" church on the internet. They were a tremendous support to me, and I ended up being caught up in a genuine revival as I witnessed miracles taking place before my eyes. One young lady walked without crutches for the first time in years after being prayed for by a visiting American preacher, the Revd Cleddie Keith. People were being set free from all kinds of conditions; it was one of the most powerful nights I've ever experienced. I suppose it wasn't too surprising since the congregation had just completed a 100-day partial fast preparing for the event. And in the midst of these extraordinary meetings, I was asked to share my own story of how my life had changed since finding Jesus inside the walls of a jail.

Somehow there was always petrol in my tank thanks to the generosity of the Christians back home, and I particularly remember the occasion when my car insurance was due and another bill also had to be paid. I needed £300, and all I had in my bank account was 3p, with another 3p in my pocket and exactly the same small amount in the car. I didn't know how I was going to get through this challenge when all I kept getting was 3p! So at the Wednesday evening service I placed my measly copper coins on the collection plate as an act of simply sowing a seed, giving everything I had, as in the Bible story about the poor widow's mite (Luke 21:1–4). I had learnt from Jesus' teaching that, if you give, it shall be given unto you!

When I came out of that service, I got a call from a Barnsley FC footballer – a member of my church back home who doesn't wish to be named. The club were playing away nearby and we agreed to meet up some forty minutes from Enfield. We got together at this restaurant and afterwards, when I returned from the toilet, there lying on the table was a pile of money amounting to exactly £300. "I just felt the Lord prompting me to give you this," he explained, knowing nothing of my plight. That was a staggering 10,000 per cent multiplication of the seed I had sown!

On another occasion, I had no money for food and hadn't eaten for a day. Then, as I was getting dressed, a £1 coin dropped out of my trainer. I was very hungry and in obvious need of some energy, and I figured it was just enough for a chocolate bar. But I felt in my spirit I should give it away instead, and placed it on the collection plate. For someone who used to rob and steal, this was quite an amazing change of lifestyle! As the plate went round, an envelope with my name on it was anonymously placed there. Inside was a £50 note. That sort of thing was happening to me almost every day.

I came back up north with a qualification that was really useful, and which formed the basis of a dynamic business model for Al's Fitness Club. So much of my first year was about getting some order, routine, and normality into the dysfunctional life I had led for so long. But I would never have got through that time without Jesus and my mentors. I was soon confident enough to step out on my own in business as a personal trainer after being invited to lead fitness classes at Dearneside Leisure Centre in Goldthorpe, near Doncaster. As well as classes, I coached individuals on a one-to-one basis and gradually built up my clientele. I realized that personal trainers can be used by God, being proactive in the community generating change; that I just need to be open as I instruct clients on diet and nutrition while at the same time engaging with people who are crying out for help on a daily basis. I hope to inspire people to be the best they can be. It's only possible by the grace of God. And you never know the impact it might have on someone.

As the New Year of 2015 dawned I decided to go on a liquid-only fast for twenty days – quite a mountain to climb for someone with a gigantic appetite like me. It wasn't easy, believe me, but I came out stronger. For example, I was developing a thicker skin, spiritually speaking, and was less easily put off from doing the right thing just because of opposition from family or otherwise. When my nephew Thomas was on a life-support machine after being seriously injured in a motorbike accident, I was not initially welcomed as I tried to pray at his bedside. I tried not to take offence but simply adopted a more subtle approach while also praying for four patients all around him – one was paralysed and another had a serious brain injury – as a result of which all four apparently made a miraculous recovery. Thomas also made a full recovery.

Meanwhile I sent messages around social media requesting prayer for another Thomas, a seriously ill premature baby. He was healed! Yes, I have seen the power of Christ demonstrated as I have prayed for people, even on the streets. I once came across an alcoholic, prayed for him on the spot, and he hasn't touched a drink since. I also prayed for a young woman who couldn't have kids – I used to sell cocaine to her partner. Now she has a second child!

Chapter 20

IN THE PINK

In November 2014 I started a fitness club for women called PinkLadies, involving a twelve-week course comprising twenty-four sessions of high-energy workouts designed to empower women to be the best they can possibly be.

I had deliberately opted for the pink emphasis – even treating myself to a bright pink jacket – to underscore the transformation in my life and outlook. People started calling me Mr Pink. Coming from my background of violence, I wanted to leave all that behind and adopt a soft approach that was a total contrast: a non-violent class enabling women to maintain weight loss and improve their fitness. I don't want to go down the male route of including martial arts and the like. In my experience, if you get groups of men together, they start fighting, and I can't handle violence any more.

It's significant that God has brought me from a laddish rugby background to running a women's fitness club. Whereas I used to view women as pieces of meat to fulfil my own desires, I now find myself treating them with kindness, gentleness, tenderness, and care. The PinkLadies were customers, yes, but also friends – valued and respected as people and certainly not objects. There was trust and respect on both sides, and the MiniPinks – the young girl members – were like my own kids.

As well as running PinkLadies, I work as a personal trainer on a one-to-one basis and have moved into areas of youth work: Al's Angels, a kids' club for three- to eleven-year-olds and a spin-off from PinkLadies; and a project for older kids (aged eleven to sixteen) involving a twelve-week fitness course with teaching on topics such as self-harm and bullying, and including a camping trip to the North York Moors.

Another positive result of my new-found faith came when my Rugby League life ban – see Chapter 11 – was first partially, then fully, lifted. Dons chaplain Dave Miller spoke in my defence at the first hearing, saying that my life had changed markedly for the better since my conversion and that, as a committed member of Bentley Baptist Church, my previously uncontrolled aggression had been rechannelled towards helping others in need.

So, I was still restricted from actually playing the game, but now at least I could spend time at the club again. I shadowed Dave for three seasons while also serving the club on match days by selling half-time draws to VIPs and directors. Although I was an ex-pro player, this was all part of the necessary process of learning humility and servanthood. When I was first told I couldn't sell half-time tickets to the players themselves (because of my life ban), I stormed off in protest, but was suitably told off by Dave. So I learnt my lesson well and sometimes stepped in as chaplain when Dave wasn't available.

When we were relegated from the Championship Division, I spent more time with the coaching staff, Gary and Pete, travelling to away games. It was during the close season that they offered me the post of assistant chaplain, with specific responsibility for player welfare and support.

As an evangelist, I couldn't have been offered a better opportunity, and the players had no issues with me sharing my faith. It blew most of their minds, because I was the bad boy of the club. My transformation was the loudest testimony they could have had. They would turn to me when they had issues – and still do – because I was an ex-player. In fact, I have probably done more chaplaincy with players away from the club than actually there.

The partial lifting was a welcome step forward, but it did effectively mean I was forced into retirement as a player. I eventually reapplied to the RFL's Appeals Panel at Brighouse in a bid to restore my reputation and enable me to return to the pitch. In allowing the appeal, the RFL said: "The panel were impressed by the considerable efforts Mr Langham has made in rehabilitating his life. He has served a four-year period not playing the game and the panel were satisfied that the sine die [playing sanction] sentence could now be rescinded."

At last I was able to resume my career as a player while continuing to mentor players under the guidance of Dave Miller. Wasting no time to get my playing career back on track, I returned to the "scene of the crime" the following week by signing for top amateur club Toll Bar, who compete in the Pennine Premier League.

In a statement to the *Doncaster Free Press*, Dons chief executive Carl Hall said:

I have known Allen for many years as a team-mate, friend and, more recently, a work colleague. He first played with us in the late 90s and broke into the first team at the back end of the season. I tried to take him away from his so-called gangster pals but, unfortunately, when the season finished he had too much spare time on his hands and dropped back into his old ways. Hooking up with his old crew, one thing led to another and he was eventually back behind bars. But he has always been a very pleasant and respectful young man around me, which is why I took a shine to him and always looked out for him, giving him some words of advice along the way. But sometimes in life you find yourself learning some very harsh lessons, which Allen has done.

I am a former player, owner and currently CEO of Doncaster RLFC, and over these last few years I have seen an immense change in Allen, to the point where we slowly introduced him back into our group at the club. Everyone is so proud of the way he has turned his life around and

*of all the good he wants to do for the community, to the
extent that we have appointed him assistant chaplain in
an official capacity – an opportunity he has taken with
both hands. I knew Allen always had a big, giving heart;
he just needed some guidance and, in the "man above", he
has found it. He might have taken the long way around,
but he has definitely become a man we are all proud of!*

And in a very personal message, he added: "You will
always be a brother to me. GOD BLESS you bro."

Yes, Carl has seen big changes in me. I once went to
his house and kicked the door in, demanding a drink. He
had to manhandle me out of his own home. Now he sees
a man of peace not needing a drink – truly born again!

Head coach Gary Thornton, who supported my
application at the appeal, chipped in:

*I have known Allen a relatively short time during my
tenure as head coach at the club. I quickly got to like this
amicable character after he came in to work alongside our
chaplain Dave Miller, but at the time I knew nothing of
his chequered past. However, having learned more about
him and got to know him better, I have been massively
impressed by the way he has turned his life around and
become the person he is today. When he asked me to
support his application to rescind the sine die [life ban]
penalty he received four years ago, I was more than happy
to help. When someone goes through the adversity and*

pain that Allen has in his life, and comes out the other side a stronger person, I could only admire his determination and belief.

The review panel were very impressed by Allen's turnaround and the way he presented himself, and it was as obvious to them, as it was to me, that this guy needed another chance. I was so pleased with their decision, because I knew how much it meant to Allen. In his own words, he felt disgraced by the sine die ruling, and to have it overturned will now give him the chance to complete his playing career and end it on his own terms. I wish him all the best and look forward to building on our relationship with Doncaster RLFC.

I was cock-a-hoop on my way back from Brighouse – absolutely thrilled. I was so looking forward to the chance of officially getting back on the pitch. All I ever wanted to be was a professional rugby player, and I was very grateful to the Appeals Panel for allowing me to be involved again in the sport I love. The support and prayers of fellow Christians and my Rugby League friends have meant so much to me. I now know that, whatever happens, I have a bright future ahead with God on my side.

Of course, I deeply regret the problems of the past which blighted my career and every aspect of my life. The Dons, in particular, have kept faith with me through the difficult times and encouraged me as my life has turned around. It was so good to be serving the club in an official capacity, giving something back after all the years they supported me.

At Toll Bar, I began by coaching the U10s with Pete. This was October 2015. And this season, after training with them twice, I was picked for the 1st XIII and duly turned out for my first match in four years as we beat Stainton of Halifax 36–20 – a great start to our new season in the Premier Division of the Pennine League, following promotion from League One after winning the League and Cup double. And we followed that up with a 68–6 trouncing of Leeds outfit Queens, who had been the team to beat for many years.

The introduction of sports chaplaincy at amateur level is now being considered, and I would be willing to take on that role too. I'd love to be the Everton chaplain – who wouldn't? But I'm learning to stick to God's agenda, not my own. I'm constantly updating my testimony on Facebook, which has become an inspiration to others. I continue to learn much about God's amazing grace, which is so undeserved.

Earlier in 2015 I had become the Dons club ambassador for White Ribbon, a campaign against domestic abuse, encouraging men not to condone or keep silent about violence to women and girls. In this capacity I attended an awareness day at the stadium of Super League club Castleford Tigers, who were playing a match against a French team in the spring of 2015. I was sitting alongside, and afterwards photographed with, West Yorkshire's Police and Crime Commissioner Mark Burns-Williamson and Shadow Home Secretary (at the time) Yvette Cooper, the local MP and a big fan! All this took place within two and a half years of that day in prison when I called on the Lord for help!

The honour of it blew my mind. I wasn't thinking, "Yes, I've arrived!"; I just felt socially inadequate, standing there in my smart suit, and humbled and blessed to be spending time in such exalted company. Mark was keen to know my thoughts on the rehabilitation of offenders. Sharing a platform with Yvette, a leading MP, was all the more remarkable, and ironic, for someone who has never been able to vote because of his prison record.

It was brought home to me that this really was the start of something new. They were recognizing the new man, the new creation that God had made.

Most amazing of all, however, was the time I hugged a judge. If there was one thing I had hated more than the police officers who would put me up in front of the judge, it was the judge himself. Judge Bennett was the Doncaster district judge who sent me down for a number of the stretches I have served. I used to get solicitors to move courts in order to avoid him. Then we met at a Football in the Community session near Sheffield, through which professional clubs offer advice and training to youngsters as part of putting something back into the local community. We ended up hugging each other after discovering we were both born-again Christians.

Only God could have done that! Here was a man I had despised, but now I felt nothing but love for him. Jesus had unlocked the raging anger and bitterness in my heart that led to so much trouble and strife.

With hindsight, I now see that he was doing God's business in delivering justice. If he hadn't sent me down, I could well have ended up permanently homeless in London. I was applying for a year's rehabilitation when I got a long prison sentence instead. I lost hope at that point, and everything went downhill. But when I reached the end of my tether in prison, God stepped in. So we can see how he works for our good in every situation, because he brought me through in the end.

Meanwhile, I found out an important thing about being a chaplain. When you're chaplain of a place, you take on the spiritual war over it. Things were going wrong at the club – illnesses, injuries, even deaths. I really assigned some prayer to it, and it was revealed that the owner had let a spiritualist go round with a crystal. There was a "Death Wall" – a memorial wall for anyone who died associated with the club. I felt really uncomfortable there; I discerned evil spirits clinging to it. So I went to pray around the club – around the seats, around the offices, at both ends of the pitch – and it shifted. But for that to happen, I paid a cost. The atmosphere around me changed; things were going wrong. I hit financial difficulties and problems with my family. My weaknesses were being attacked. I had taken on the personal burden of dealing with powers and principalities without the spiritual authority to do so, and the support of other chaplains. My God-given ministry was for the players, not to carry out spiritual warfare.

As usual, I was doing it on my own. I was still in the process of re-establishing myself as a person. This was just one indication that God still had a whole lot more work to do in me.

As I write this, I think back to four years ago when I posted a status update online: *Happy, happy, happy. Thanks for backing me.* I'd just got out from court after being in prison for the seventh time; a place where I'd wasted seven accumulative years, spanning most of my adult life.

I had been a little, lost, hurting boy, trapped in an eighteen-stone, steroid-filled, violent man's body. I was broken. I'd hit a point of no return. I was an embarrassment and deemed no good; a failure as a father and as a man! I cried out at a point of desperation, "God, if you are real, if you are hearing me, put a dove outside my window." I was on my knees, tears running down my face, completely desperate and contemplating how I might take my own life. I couldn't cope with who and what I'd become. I was a mentally insane, chronically depressed, drug-addicted, drug-dealing failure.

God answered my cries and sent the dove. He came into that cell and pulled me out of the darkness of shame, bitterness, and pain. He poured his love into my heart.

He healed my mind and set me free from the cycle of destruction, and equipped me to carry on with life; to not give up and die, but to live! To be a father, to be respected, to live a normal life. To be a message of hope.

I have many failings and have got it wrong so many times, but if there's one thing I'm certain of, it is that God is real! He is alive and he loves you.

Four years on from walking out of that prison, we hit the milestone of the hundredth member signing up to Pink Ladies. That means everything to me, and I ask all my ladies to have a celebratory glass or two of their favourite tipple, because without you none of it would have been possible.

I love you all so very much, so once more I want to say: *Happy, happy, happy. Thanks for backing me.*

Thank you, Jesus, for your love, your peace, your joy, your grace, and your mercy.

Open your heart. Jesus loves you. Ask him in.

Chapter 21

PRIDE COMES BEFORE A FALL

Over Christmas 2014 I decided to feed the homeless, remembering that I had once been in that position myself. I put a message on Facebook inviting anyone who had nowhere to go to come over to my place. As a result, I was able to collect enough donations of food, toys, and clothing for fourteen families. When a Barnsley family received their gift, they said it was a "miracle", adding, "They won't even give us a cup of tea in this street." It was a one-man crusade to share the real message of Christmas. And in fact I was blessed in return. My sister turned up with a hamper full of food for us, and someone gave me £50 to spend on each of my three children for Christmas. So much stuff came in I had to store it in a friend's garage. Looking back, however, I realize it had not been a purely selfless venture, but was based on a need within me. I had no money or food in the fridge before this, and the kids would have had no Christmas presents.

I had been basking in the warmth of God's goodness while enjoying a degree of consistency – in terms of overall well-being, behaviour, and relationships – that I hadn't known before. I was praying at a deeper level and seeing miracles of healing after laying hands on folk. But I was heading for a fall. I was acting as if I knew best and didn't need any help or guidance. I was reaching out to people from my own unresolved pain; it became my new "fix", serving my need, not theirs. It was about me when it should have been about them. It was effectively for my glory, not God's. I was getting obsessive, simply replacing my old addictions with new ones. There was a reason Jesus sent his disciples out in twos. I was buzzing all the time, but like a busy bee, no longer a man at peace with himself.

The problem was that I was getting too cocky and sure of myself, which allowed pride to get a grip. Pride isn't so much about sticking out your chest, declaring how wonderful you are – that is arrogance – as believing that you are the master of your own fate. Even though I was always aware that God was with me, I wouldn't think to check with anyone else (particularly my mentors) if they felt I was hearing right; I would simply act on my feelings. So if I saw someone who was sick, I would rush in to pray for them without first checking to see if God wanted me to be involved. I would be rushing around telling everybody that Jesus is the answer – which of course he is – without seeking wisdom about precisely how to go about it in a given context. I was too busy "doing"; I wasn't listening. I had become proud of my own gifting as an evangelist. But "fools rush in where angels fear to tread" (Alexander Pope) and "pride goes before destruction, a haughty spirit before a fall" (Proverbs 16:18). I needed to humble myself before God, which meant that I needed to be far more accountable, especially to the church elders and those who were discipling me. God has created a structure in the church to protect us from ourselves and our worst follies, so that we're not just doing things out of zeal, but from a God-given knowledge about what is required in a given circumstance.

I began to recognize this ugliness of pride when I went down to London for another college course, this time to qualify as a sports chaplain. I heard that an acquaintance was in the area wanting to meet up for prayer, I didn't think to check with the Lord if this was OK; I simply figured it must be God because of the circumstances of this guy being close by. As it happened, I was badly out of my depth when we met up.

I didn't know the guy very well – we'd communicated on social media. I told his pastor, and his pastor told me straight up, "Don't get involved." I ignored that advice. We met up when I was straight out of a fast, which I broke by feasting on sandwiches and crisps, and started on a Langham sightseeing tour. On a visit to the West End, where I had once slept on the streets as a member of the homeless fraternity, I'd discovered places that were "named after me" – Langham Place, the Langham Hotel. Now I wanted to see them!

Very soon my acquaintance began to show very strange behaviour, grabbing his genitals, moaning in pain, and asking me to help him. "My nuts are hurting so bad!" he said.

As far as I was concerned, this was just getting in the way of the sightseeing. "Listen, we'll deal with that in two minutes, mate – let me just enjoy Langham Square, right?"

We got on the tram back to his flat and he got louder and louder with the same complaint, so that I was having to hush him up in front of everyone. As soon as I walked into his flat, I finally started to feel fearful. It just didn't feel right to be there. I started to panic. What should I do? Well, pray, of course! So I did, like I had the authority to make it all better with a click of my fingers. But I didn't, and it finally got to the point where I just had to get out of there. I made my excuses and went.

Which brings me back to authority. It was a very scary lesson about the consequences of not listening to people's advice. The pastor obviously knew something I didn't, and warned me off. This guy had problems, but they were for his church and pastor to handle, not me. Right from the way I broke my fast, I broke the rules of engagement. It wasn't my domain. Pride had revealed itself, masked by the desire to help somebody.

I subsequently became quite dispirited, but I still wasn't learning any lessons. I got into a few tangles with young women – again believing God was leading me through feelings and circumstances when in fact it was a trap of the devil to cause me to sin. And with PinkLadies taking off, I got carried away imagining myself driving a pink Land Rover, having already built up colour-coordinated stationery and other accessories. Once again I was mistaking emotion for the Holy Spirit's leading, and I became a mental and physical wreck as a result.

Sometimes when we believe we're doing the right things, we can end up burning the candle at both ends. We're up early in the morning for prayer and it might be midnight before we get to sleep. We're not looking after ourselves. We believe that we're in God's will because we're doing good things, and we're mentally drained because we're taking on everyone's burdens, giving them permission to enter our lives.

Well, stop and look at Jesus' blueprint. Everything he ever did was birthed out of prayer. When he chose the disciples, he spent all night in prayer first (Luke 6:12–13). I can't remember any time I spent the whole night in prayer about a decision. When he was going to the cross, not only did he go and pray and cry out to the Father; he asked all his disciples to pray with him as well. Also, remember God doesn't expect us to run ourselves into the ground for him. We might have to do long hours at times for certain things, but God sets a flow on it. When we find ourselves absolutely mentally and physically walloped, it's usually a key indicator that we're out of the will of God.

I was finding it hard to humble myself and ask for help because I felt I was being a nuisance and I didn't want to share the fact that I'd been struggling. So I became all the busier, telling everyone why they needed Jesus while inside I felt deep pain, loneliness, and shame for going off the rails. I knew I was on a slippery slope, even reverting to cannabis to fill the void and numb the agony of feeling so condemned.

I was deceptive with my mentors by confessing different misdemeanours with each of them without telling the whole story, but they found me out. Finally, by a process of elimination and comparing of notes, they came to the conclusion that I needed to come under some strict discipline. They banned me from public ministry, such as speaking and praying for others. I was restricted to washing cups until I learnt to be properly accountable for everything I did.

I had forgotten that as Christians we're in a constant state of spiritual warfare. I broke down and confessed all my failures to Bruce. Bruce identified strongholds of my mind, such as hypersensitivity and desperate insecurity, as he prayed over me with tears, and I sensed a power in the room that day as I felt something lift off me.

I needed to go through all this in order to understand the fear of the Lord. I got so scared at one point I thought the Holy Spirit had left me. Things really opened up after this breakthrough. Alice came to live with me, the club offered me a new post, and other surprises were in store.

Chapter 22

RELIVING MY YOUTH

It was only when I began working on this book that I realized there were some deep-rooted issues that had not yet been dealt with. I was just glossing over the unpleasant facts of my early life, because I was reluctant to really face up to my past. I also came across a book dealing with the healing of memories, some of which clearly hadn't been dealt with despite earlier deliverance from serious strongholds relating to sex and violence. This kind of pain needed to be replaced by "rivers of living water" from the Spirit of Jesus (John 7:38).

So, in 2015, I took this up with our new pastor, another Dave, David Augur. At our first meeting, David asked me why I was so angry – and I defensively replied, "I'm not!" I distinctly remembered God taking anger from me. That had been my very first supernatural deliverance, my first evidential transformation, right at the start of my Christian journey, in that cell in Armley.

But "anger" was definitely the word he had been given, and as we talked, we realized that what had been taken from me in Armley was *rage*. Different thing. Rage is what makes us explode, like I used to. Anger lurks more quietly in the background and corrodes us slowly from within. I had nursed anger for so long that it had become a stronghold in my life. Physically I was out of prison, but mentally and emotionally I was still bound up. These strongholds needed to be cast out with the authority of Jesus.

So, David and I scheduled six sessions of serious prayer for emotional healing. At each one of these, we would work through a particular issue. Mum, Dad, sex... I hadn't properly dealt with the pain of the loss of my mum, the rejection of my dad walking out on us, or having kids out of wedlock. This was probably going to be the hardest time I had faced so far as a Christian.

The first session dealt with my memories of my mother. The first memory of all to come under the spotlight was me finding my mum dead. Ever since then I had been angry with the woman who had died on me and left me. I loved her so much that I hated her. I needed to forgive my mum for dying.

David took me through my memories of the time, which I described in chapter 3: finding my mum dead on the settee, and my brother-in-law, Pat, turning up at the house and then holding my hand in reassurance as he took me through to see her. Back then I'd been told to dry my tears, but now, more than twenty years later, a tear came down my cheek, and I broke down crying. We started to pray around that, and it was as though a big cloud lifted off me. There was a horrible feeling in my hands which then ran through my whole body, and I knew that *something* had left me.

I didn't receive my fullest healing over my mum for another couple of years, but we'll come to that, and in the meantime the work had begun.

David and I reconvened for our second session the next week, and this time the subject was my dad. A distorted experience of our dad can mean a distorted vision of God, and healing one heals the other.

My dad hadn't been around for most of my childhood, but he hadn't vanished completely. I remembered a time when he had promised to pick me up one weekend. I was so excited! I had fantasized so long about having a dad and normal parents. I told all my friends and anyone who would listen.

We arranged to meet at a phone box on Barnsley Road. And guess what, it was a no-show. Eventually I called the number he had given me. It was a pub. "Sorry," the guy at the other end said, "he's working this weekend."

That little boy felt his heart break. He sat down on the pavement, and cried, and cried. Now, as I remembered this with David, I started to convulse and choke. David was given insight that there was a spirit of abandonment in me, and he ordered it to come out. It was the first time I had heard of spirits being mentioned, but I woke up the next day with peace in my heart.

Since then, my dad and I have reconciled, but I have

had to get to grips with the fact that he could never be a father. He's over seventy – he doesn't have the capacity and our expectations are just too far apart. My need and what he can give me are two opposite things.

He has publicly declared his pride in me, but because he was away for so long, and because he only returned when a relationship he had thought was forever broke down unexpectedly, it is difficult to bridge the gap between us. I honour him as much as possible – I arranged his seventieth birthday party; I take him to hospital when he needs it – but a day-to-day relationship is hard. That is the place I just have to be in. The child who desperately needs a father's love will only get it from the Father of the fatherless. My biological father doesn't have the ability to be a dad, but I'm accepted in the family of Christ. God has said, "Never will I leave you; never will I forsake you" (Hebrews 13:5).

Our third session was focused on sexual issues. So much in my life had totally distorted what God meant as a wonderful gift to his children. I equated sex with love, love with sex. When my mum died, I was a teenager, fourteen, nearly fifteen, and I wanted to do sexual things because I needed comfort. When I felt frightened, I would want somebody in my bed to sleep with because I was fearful. I thought that if someone's in my bed then I'm loved and I don't need to be frightened.

Porn had been a norm in my life, and I'd been exposed to it from early on. It was never seen as degrading to women – it was just there. Someone I babysat for had a collection on VHS. I'd get my mates round to watch it, with the kids upstairs.

As a child I'd been violently assaulted and sexually abused – and I am actually thankful that if I had to follow one route or the other myself, I went down the one of being violent rather than being an abuser! I wrestled with sexuality as a young man. Meanwhile, I had issues with black people because of my abuse from a black person, and with gays because of my experiences on the streets of London. And there was still the haunting childhood memory of a more sinister abuse, where all I remember for sure is the trilby hat.

I confessed the separate relationships that had led to my three children being born out of wedlock, and to many more sexual encounters with both genders. This was one of the most violent deliverance sessions I've had. I was thrown to the floor, writhing, choking on saliva, eyes bulging. The pain was excruciating. My kidneys felt they were being ripped out and at one point it felt like my back was going to snap.

Whatever had happened to cause such pain, it had an effect. Down below just didn't work any more after that. I had no more sexual desire of any kind. Something had been broken. This was my first sustained period without sexual activity since I first became active.

But the most significant outcome of this session was that something spoke out of me. It said, "There's hundreds of us."

My abused, battered young body had been opened up to all kinds of influences, before and after birth. The child of unmarried parents with a history of paedophilia, abuse and incest, down both bloodlines. Then, after birth, trauma, abuse, the occult, my criminal lifestyle, false religions. They had all opened doors for dark forces into my life, and now they gave themselves away. The demon-possessed man that Jesus meets in Mark 5 tells him, "My name is Legion... for we are many." Maybe I got off lightly with "only" hundreds.

David, on the other hand, had never seen this scale of manifestation before, and even though he didn't question the deliverance, he did query the hundreds bit, which hurt me.

At this point we took a break for a while, which was a relief because those first three sessions had been pretty heavy duty. For our next session, we went for a walk and prayed. I confessed that I was getting paralytic fears, especially at night. I would lie there and fear... everything. I knew I was helpless and couldn't do a thing about it. David discerned a spirit of fear in me and ordered it out.

Around this time, my cousin produced the Hennessey family Bible – that's my mum's family line. This was the kind of massive old tome that is passed down from generation to generation, listing who married who and had which kids and when they were born and died. It went back to the 1800s and, as far as I was concerned, it was just littered with death. It stank of it. And that was my line.

But in the fifth session, Jesus revealed his lineage to me instead. Matthew 1 is the passage in the Bible that everyone skips over – begat, begat, begat. All those ancestors, including a prostitute, a murderer, a polygamist... and many others besides. Jesus showed it to me like a big scroll above me while I knelt at the foot of the cross. Now I saw that I wasn't of the Langham or the Hennessey lineage. I knew I was adopted into God's family; but in fact, it goes deeper than that. I'm *grafted* into his lineage. I'm his son, God's son. I'm part of his family. My identity is in Christ.

I don't have the Hennessey Bible any more. I burnt it. A whirlwind of smoke came off it, pouring away into nothing. That's the Hennessey lineage, done.

Solidifying my identity in Christ helped to release me from the self-destructive tendency in my personality. But straight away there was a setback – part of the endless, ongoing fight that always happens when someone is making spiritual progress. It was the end of that relationship with David. David began to distance himself – he thought I was too much to handle. It wasn't just the stuff coming out of me. I was imposing on his life, phoning and texting too much, to the point that he had to put boundaries around when I could ring. All of a sudden David and his wife, who at one point had been almost Dad and Mum to me, became almost strangers. I felt abandoned and slipped into sin.

But I was still under David's authority as my pastor, and so I confessed the sin to David. He immediately placed me under discipline and asked me for my keys to the church. I couldn't understand what was happening, but God gave David exactly the right words to say.

"You're unbalanced with church stuff, Allen," he told me. "You need to start finding friendships. Relationships. Hobbies."

It was a Christian way of saying, "Get a life", though neither of us had any idea where it would lead.

Chapter 23

UNETERNAL LIFE

It was early summer 2016. I had the promise of eternal life, but God, speaking through David, wanted me to have an uneternal, mortal life as well.

I know now why. I was still in a place of unravelling from old to new. From baptism onwards, my life has been a time of seasons: a time for every purpose, as Ecclesiastes puts it. My traumas were a bit like being shot. The bullet goes straight through and out again, but it leaves a residue behind. The residue must still be dealt with. A process of deliverance and refining of my character had really started to happen, but it was in contradiction to how I was living, still always on the go. With my maverick attitude, I still felt I knew best. I needed to slow down and take time to let it happen.

I'd always been a keen fisherman, ever since my days of bunking off to fish at Cusworth Hall. Still a bit dazed and confused over what I was getting from David, I went off and – still only in my late thirties – managed to join an over-50s fishing club at Barnburgh Lakes, near Doncaster.

So, was this what Christ had brought me to, after my years of wild living?

I was sitting on my fishing box and pondering this, when my phone rang. It was a lady called Trish and she introduced herself as the Head of Youth Offender Services in Grimsby.

"My husband told me he doesn't like you," she told me. Good start. "But we've heard what you're doing and I think we need you. We're running a summer arts project for young people, here in Grimsby. I'd like to invite you to come and talk to our young people, and tell them your story."

So I did.

The project staff took my breath away. The time and energy and love they put into the young people in their care took me back to my own youth offender officer. For the first time, I began to understand why certain key people in my life had done what they did. I had looked at them suspiciously, wondering what their game was. They were authority, so there had to be some kind of twist. But at last I saw that there had been no ulterior motive, just love and kindness.

I talked to the kids. I interviewed each of them, one-to-one, and had a chat, offering encouragement, motivation, and a bit of understanding. They were really receptive to what I said. There was a presentation of a photography project that they had just done, and it was heart-breaking. Dark, ominous backgrounds, and brutal, hurting imagery – the photos showed how the kids saw themselves through society's eyes. They weren't labelled as kids, just as problems.

I told my story, leaving the staff and the young people and the VIP visitors open-mouthed. Once they'd got over that, they asked if I had more – and I realized that I did.

Two years earlier, after my first ever time of prayer and fasting, God had given me the outline of what is now the Steps to Freedom course. There was no structure yet, just a framework based on my own experiences to reach out to young people in crisis who need a helping hand to freedom and stability. I realized, as I described it to my listeners – who liked what they heard – that ideas aren't finished articles. I needed the nuts and bolts to deliver something.

Even I realized this couldn't be done in a day by one maverick Christian. The project would be with high-risk offenders, so it needed virtually a one-to-one staff-to-young person ratio. It had to be developed by a team, using the gifts that are available in different people. So, the first obstacle to overcome was that I had learn to share my ideas with others.

I met with David, who could see that I'd got something decent, and we put the project together. In contrast to me and my impulsiveness, David is very structured and organized, and we were graced with great staff. The Company Secretary and Company Chairman were both elders at the church.

We put the project into a format presentable to management, with a workbook and timetable to deliver the course in the six weeks before Christmas 2016.

It was great for the kids, great for the staff, great for Grimsby, but for all the good we were doing, I found I was coming away from each session once again struggling with trauma. At the first session, we had a disclosure of criminal activity. At the second, we had to bring the police in because we learnt of a young person's link with organized crime. We had a disclosure of intrafamilial abuse, and this was all in the first couple of sessions. I was revisiting places of hurt in myself that hadn't been dealt with fully. My deliverance wasn't done.

As the project was winding up, around that Christmas, I got a random Facebook message about Tent City Doncaster – a homeless campsite set up in in the heart of town. I sprang straight into action, and put a video on Facebook urging members of the public to donate supplies. I did a phone interview with a local reporter and it went online. Within the hour, I had received a death threat from an organization called Fightback.

My crime? I had "entered an occupied site". It turned out Tent City wasn't a genuine homeless site; it was part of a far-Left anti-austerity movement with links to high places in London. I'd stepped right into an area I wasn't meant to be in. Also, if I'd bothered to ask, I'd have soon learnt that Tent City went right against the Church of Doncaster's own system for helping the homeless. So I had upset the church *and* the far Left. I was still acting like a maverick.

I quickly deleted the video and put out a second appeal, to direct donations to Riverside, the official Doncaster homeless project. I also refunded donations that had already come in via PayPal.

But this only dealt with the short-term damage. The same day, Bruce said he could no longer mentor me – he felt it had reached a conclusion. David had already taken a back seat, as Steps to Freedom took off. It was the end of that kind of counselling and deliverance, and I was on the edge of a breakdown. I put a video on the Steps to Freedom website to say as much. I said I couldn't carry on and I was taking some time out.

Straightaway I got waves of support from the public, and one person sent me a gift of £500: not to go to any charity, not for Steps to Freedom, but specifically for me to take time out with the kids. We went to Blackpool for the weekend. This was the end of 2016.

As we went into 2017, I knew I needed clarity and direction from the Lord. There were still threats to my life and character assassination going on. At home, there was a lot of family tension, with people not talking to me, and issues with my daughter. And behind all this, I was still troubled by that "hundreds of us". My support network was gone. I felt God had moved everyone from my life. Now I had to stand on my own two feet for the first time, and seek him.

So, I finished the project, and did my last feed at Riverside. I wrapped up 2016 with the Big Feed, where we fed about 200 people that Christmas, over four projects. Even then, I realized I wasn't really doing it for them. I was trying to meet a need in other people that had already been met. They were already in shelters, already being fed. No, I was just doing this for myself, because if I wasn't doing something over Christmas then I would be alone.

On 1 January 2017, I started a ten-day Daniel fast.

And then I went to Wales.

Chapter 24

DELIVER US FROM EVIL

High in Pembrokeshire's Preseli Hills is Ffald-y-Brenin, a Christian retreat house founded in 1984. The name means "Sheepfold of the King". What were crumbling farm buildings have been converted into accommodation, meeting rooms, and a chapel where the bedrock of the mountain comes up through the floor. It is a place of amazing peace in the heart of the mountains. Your signal fades away as you approach it, but it's not just phone contact that gets left behind.

The leaders pronounced a blessing on me as I arrived, which is their usual thing. And straightaway I lost my wallet – couldn't find it anywhere. This struck me as an odd outcome to a blessing.

But a blessing isn't right if we aren't right, and as the day went on and I got into the Ffald-y-Brenin swing, the reason began to settle on me. It was unforgiveness lying heavy within me. All this hurt, all this rejection – I wasn't handing it over to God; I wasn't even trying to do anything positive about it myself. I was just hoarding it up in my heart.

It came to a head as I sat in the chapel that night. I kind of drifted off to sleep – that semi-conscious state where you're neither one thing nor the other. And I saw a message marked out on the chapel floor in pebbles – "I forgive".

I thought it was just part of the design of the chapel, along with the natural bedrock, except that when I went back to the chapel after a good night's sleep, it wasn't there.

After that, I went to the foot of the cross – literally. There is a large wooden cross at the top of the valley. I went there owning the unforgiveness in my heart that stopped my blessing being received, and as I sat there I tried forgiving everyone I could think of in the name and strength of Jesus, dredging up every name I could from the depths of my memory.

The next day, as I was due to leave, one of the leaders called me back for another blessing. This was unusual, but whatever, I thought. They also paid my fees, since I still couldn't find my wallet. Then I got into my car, and for some reason felt moved to lift up the lid of the central console. And there was my wallet.

I said that the mobile phone signal fades away as you approach Ffald-y-Brenin, so the obvious opposite of that is that as you drive away, it comes back. My phone started to buzz, and buzz, and buzz again. Booking after booking was coming in for PinkLadies, in record numbers. It was the start of something new. I went off full of energy and blessing, and stuff started coming together.

But if you think I actually learned anything from this encounter with God's forgiveness and healing, you haven't been paying attention.

I longed for a prison ministry, reaching out to those poor souls who were where I had once been. Bruce arranged for me to visit Isis, a Young Offenders' Institution in Woolwich, next door to Belmarsh, where I had spent so much of my life for the wrong reasons. I duly left Doncaster at quarter to five in the morning. At the petrol station I half-filled up my diesel car with regular petrol before I realized my mistake. So I put half a tank of diesel on top of that and just set off anyway. By the time I got as far as Nottingham the car was in limp mode.

But the Lord had other ideas. As I pulled over on the motorway, I just said, "Lord, if it's your will then get me to London to share my story with the prisoners."

I banged my hand on the wheel and said, "In the name of Jesus," and that car jumped into life. It miraculously got to London and back again, which is a virtual impossibility, because when you put petrol into a diesel engine, it just doesn't work.

I went in and shared my testimony, which was really well received. The lady who runs the ministry team down there said, "The love of Jesus radiates out of this man."

After that, I did a long fast for Lent, craving the superpower of the Spirit that would let me keep on changing the world. I joined a marriage group online, hoping to meet my wife – but instead I met and joined a fasting group. Soon after that I was on a twenty-one-day liquid fast, right on top of the Lenten one. Well, I thought, if that's what God wants…

But things were piling up. I went to town with my new income from my increased business, settling my debts and doing my house up – which left me with no money. I had plans for Steps to Freedom but I didn't run them past the board. It was all signed and sealed and delivered on behalf of a local school, Years 7 to 10, but I was so impulsive that it ended up as borderline misappropriation – in fact, the board were ready to call the police. In the end they disciplined me.

Meanwhile, I was still struggling with my weaknesses so that fasting felt like a punishment, not a means to achieve God's end. "I do not understand what I do," wrote Paul. "For what I want to do I do not do, but what I hate I do" (Romans 7:15). That was so right.

With money gone and problems escalating, there was one obvious answer to me – head back to Ffald-y-Brenin. It can be dangerous to associate blessing with a place, but as far as I could see, I'd lost my blessing, and there was only one place I'd get it back.

I turned up at Ffald-y-Brenin for the second time, out of the blue and without a reservation, on day nineteen of my twenty-one-day fast. I had a firm agenda in mind: renew or rediscover my blessing, get the power of the Holy Spirit, leave again to go off and do miracles – just like last time, but this time even better and with nothing going wrong once I'd left. And if I found I didn't have the strength for it – well, then, I'd fast until I did.

I suppose a conviction that strong gives God something to latch onto. I sat in a service in the chapel, soaking up the peace of the place, and God's conviction settled on me, replacing my own: a lot of sins, and a bad agenda. My mindset, making it all about me, was about as wrong as wrong gets. God doesn't work like that. God's power is a gift to the weak, and I needed to be weak for God's power to work in me.

I went back to the cross, on foot, my mind whirling. It's one thing to have it made very clear you're wrong – but not so obvious as to what is right. I went to pray and ask the Lord for someone to talk and confess to.

He gave me one of the leaders, a guy called Steve. I bumped into him as I walked back from the cross. I could literally tell him, "You could be the answer to my prayer! Can I sit down and share with you?"

I talked, he listened, for so long that he picked up a bit of sunburn. I confessed and bared my soul for about two and a half hours.

"Have you ever heard of soul ties?" Steve asked me. I hadn't, and he recommended a book on them. I got it from their library and read it, sitting on the mountainside, and filled up my iPad with stuff that came to me. Soul ties are formed when people become close in some way. For instance, the Bible talks about people becoming one: one flesh, one spirit. That is through marriage, which is good. But people who come together through illicit sex may have a soul tie that harms them. I had shared close, sinful lifestyles, giving soul ties plenty of opportunities to form. I'd let in entities that were still there and needed dealing with. Look at the ministry of Jesus: so much of it involved casting out unclean spirits even for what looked like a simple healing.

Meanwhile, I had just turned up at Ffald-y-Brenin, and it only has so much space. After this great day there, a leader told me, very sadly, that there weren't any rooms available.

So, I got back in my car and headed back to the M4 motorway. I had tickets for a Big Church Day Out in London, and in a few hours I could be there instead.

Halfway up the motorway, about 9 p.m., my phone went.

"Allen? We have a room after all."

"I'm halfway to London!" I said.

"Ah, well," he said. "You must not have been meant to be here, so we'll leave it."

I thanked them anyway, and kept going... straight into one of the M4's more epic standstills. I don't believe that the Lord causes accidents, but I genuinely believe that sometimes things are so God-ordained that he uses circumstances so it can seem like it. After several hours of going nowhere very slowly, I pulled off at some services for a burger, because I was ravenous. It still wasn't worth rejoining the motorway after that, so I tucked myself up and fell asleep in the car. I woke up in the early hours – which is very easy to do, when you're sleeping in a car – with one name repeating in my heart, over and over. "Ffald-y-Brenin..."

I pointed my car back down the motorway and got there, running on the last fumes in my tank, in time for the 8.30 morning service.

It turned out that the room availability was because of a cancellation by a pastor and his family, so it was a double room! A double portion, as the Bible says. The rooms at Ffald-y-Brenin are very simple – whitewashed and almost cell-like, with views of the garden and the hills. I sat down in this beautiful room, so full of peace and quiet and grace, and broke down.

I went downstairs. There was a group of about twenty there, on retreat together. We had tea and coffee and chatted. It was a wonderful family feeling, and I felt I had to share why I'd come to Ffald-y-Brenin in the first place. So I stood up and I said, "My intention coming down here after a period of prayer and fasting was to get the power of the Spirit. I've realized my agenda was wrong. I've realized, being here, that I need to become weak in order for the power of God to work through me. I believe I'm dealing with soul ties, and I'd like you to support and pray me through them."

We started to pray – and I went to the floor, convulsing. I started to manifest: a demonic entity or an unclean spirit, whatever language you use. You see, this wasn't just any random group. They were a group called to the deliverance ministry and who were well versed in doing deliverance drills. Their pastor was a gynaecological surgeon, who did his day job with the support and back-up of a well-trained team. That was how they did it here. Someone held me down, gently but firmly, while I writhed. Someone knelt by me, wiping my face of spit and sweat. Someone read Scripture over me, someone got the children out of the way. A lady called Beth sung Graham Kendrick's "Holy Overshadowing" in a sweet, angelic voice while her husband played acoustic guitar. It was the first time this group had really worked together this way in practice. With their pastor's professional background, they called me their first baby!

That day, I was delivered from a spirit of pride – publicly, openly, and in a service – the best way to get rid of pride!

Later, after a time for rest, reflection, and recovery, I drove with the pastor to town, to get food for dinner. I said, "I don't think it's finished." At the time, I had no idea how much more work there was to do – apart from that utterance, "There's hundreds of us", which was always at the back of my mind. And, since then, I know at least a hundred demonic entities have come out of my body.

He agreed.

"No, you're right there, but we couldn't have done much more. That was enough for today. We'll go into it more, probably later tonight, or tomorrow." He had discerned that there was more to come, but that was it for now.

In fact, that was it for several days. In my usual way, I wanted to get on with it, but somehow we seemed to be interrupted every time. I had an iPad full of stuff that I'd written on the mountainside to get through, but every time we got close to it, there seemed to be some kind of opposition, to the point where I was getting desperate.

Finally, on the group's last day there, after the chapel service, the pastor said to the congregation, "I want you people to pray." Meanwhile, three other people led me into another room, and sat down and started to work through the stuff that was on the iPad. As they prayed, I started manifesting again and this time they commanded out spirit after spirit after spirit, over a good hour or more. There was coughing, being sick, saliva, groaning, shouting, laughing, squeals. At one stage I couldn't see – a strangling spirit, maybe a python spirit, was making my eyes bulge out of my head. They had to pray over my eyes, reading the scripture in Mark 8 where Jesus heals a blind man. He sees men for the first time but says they look like trees, walking around. That is how it was for me. For a while, until my sight returned properly, I could only see shadows.

I can't put a name to all the spirits that came out that day, but one I can identify was the spirit of poverty that I've mentioned before. It came out of me like black tar in my saliva, as I coughed and retched. The leaders told me later that it was the foulest smell they had ever known, and the room had to be aired out after. I couldn't smell anything – I'd virtually passed out by then.

I now know that I had to go through all that – driving away, coming back – for God to work. I had gone there expecting God to jump to my desires. Well, he was doing it in his time and his way. But the major lesson was to see spiritual warfare intensifying to a whole new level.

Chapter 25

AMAZING GRACE

It was as if I'd been through a major operation – and I had, spiritually speaking. With an experience as intense as the one I'd had at Ffald-y-Brenin, I needed to recuperate. This comes from the top. How many times do we read of Jesus going off to be alone? I should have spent two months coming down after Wales.

I spent two days on the settee. I wanted that experience in our own congregation, and I wanted it straight away. I came back to church with a fresh heart, but all I did was rub people up the wrong way, telling folk who had been doing their work for years how they should do it my way: "We need to do this; we need to do that; we need to put in a discipleship programme."

The first sermon after I came back I listened to in disbelief as the speaker outlined a new vision for the church – which was all the stuff that I had already decided we should be doing. Now, I know I should have been delighted. If I believed the vision for this work came from God, then it would be to God's glory for it to happen, so why shouldn't the congregation also share it? Instead I just felt resentful that someone else was having the good ideas too.

David apologized to me for doubting the manifestations, because since then, he'd seen the same in somebody else he was ministering to. That apology gave me a release to get stuck into my projects, but because I went at it in such a wrong way, and on top of the resentment I was already feeling, inevitably I experienced rejection and hurt. Even if people were politely and reasonably trying to calm me down, rejection and hurt is what it felt like.

I responded to the hurt by eating. I ballooned up to twenty-one stone. Even with all that manifesting back at Ffald-y-Brenin, something – in fact, several things – had still not been dealt with. I felt I needed comfort, and eating seemed a lesser evil than turning to drink or drugs or sex. The fact is, something else had control of me. Self-control is one of the fruits of the Holy Spirit. Quench that and you quench the Spirit.

You needed to know me well to see anything wrong, though. On the surface, everything seemed fine – I was still cruising on the blessing I had received at Ffald-y-Brenin. In particular, my longed-for prison ministry was taking off – despite my best efforts to stop it.

After my success at Isis, the chaplain of Doncaster prison – a little closer to home than Woolwich – called me up.

"Allen, I'd like to invite you to come and minister…"

Great!

"… to the Rule 43s."

Ah.

The Rule 43s are prisoners on protection, kept apart from the rest of the population. Any inmate can request it; the ones who do usually need it. The murderers. The rapists. The paedophiles. The people I did not want to minister to.

I'd done everything else – I'd fed the homeless, I'd done appeals and Crisis for Families, I'd done everything I possibly could to serve the Lord and meet the needy – but if I had to go back into jail, I wanted to preach to the "normal" prisoners. In my own time, the Rule 43s were fair game for violent assault with blades, hot water, whatever it took to get at them. Offenders might come onto the wing with a cover story to hide the facts of their crime, but it would come out – sometimes with a tip-off from a prison officer, or their last jail. Once, in Belmarsh, there was a rapist on the wing: we covered the cameras up and savagely attacked him in his cell. He was as close to not being here as a person could possibly get.

That was my past with the Rule 43s. So, I made my apologies to the chaplain – but as soon as I came off the phone I knew I'd done wrong. I picked up the phone, rang straight back, and said I'd come.

I was going to go in with Bruce, but for some reason there was a delay with renewing his security clearance, so for the next six weeks it was just me and the chaplain. Over those six weeks, the Lord gave me knowledge and insight as I preached to both normal prisoners and the ones on protection. At the first sermon I preached, I received the word "victim". There was this bunch of angry men, all convicted of heinous crimes, and all I could see was the word victim over them. And not all of them were paedophiles or murderers – like the guy in a wheelchair who had been disabled in the crash that had killed his best friend. Not only was he dealing with the disability, but he'd lost his friend, and on top of all that, he was looking at a hefty prison sentence.

What I would notice initially would be a tear leaking out. Tears are words unspoken. When I saw the tears, I knew there would be a waterfall coming. The dam can just burst.

The song "Amazing Grace" is a testimony to how awesome God's nature is. John Newton, who wrote it, had been a slave trader. He realized he was a wretch, and how amazing God was to set him free. When a person has spent most of their adult life in prison, beaten people up, harmed them, maimed them, sold drugs, and terrorized communities, they believe they're a wretch, that they're not worth anything, that they're not part of society. To see a man break down and cry, and get the revelation of who God is, when I know that man has systematically abused children most of his life, has changed my whole perspective of grace. To have the opportunity to go into those dark places, to minister to people of such deprived and depraved backgrounds, showed me the grace that was over my life, and the grace that the Lord was teaching me.

Meanwhile, I wasn't going to church, my own church – or if I was, it was as little as I possibly could. I continued to rub people up the wrong way with my constant requests to support my ministry: "Can you bless us with some study materials and help?", and I felt hurt and rejected by the inevitable response. Going into prison now was an excuse not to go there – until it turned out that the prison ministry wouldn't last anyway. I had a dream of climbing through a side window of a house that I knew. The room was full of wine bottles – empty, because the head chaplain at prison had drunk it all. Jesus' first miracle was to provide wine, but what the dream told me was that coming through the side window was illegal entry. I wasn't meant to be there. Soon after that, the prison ministry ended.

In one way, the outreach of the ministry was a fantastic thing – but, with hindsight, I also think God permits things to happen to deliver lessons. It's all about divine timing, and the timing wasn't right for that one.

David left our church unexpectedly in late 2017. In fact, half of that local community, people who'd been there for years, were suddenly leaving, and it was as if the foundation of the church had been smashed.

It got to the point where I was just surviving each day. Get up, survive, go back to bed. I had some prayer life but I was just ticking the boxes. I didn't feel welcome at church. I'd stopped my own physical training, and I was getting fatter and fatter. The Steps to Freedom board decided that they couldn't support me with my bad attitude, and resigned. It came to a head as the year came to an end and I lost my driving licence. It wasn't any one, big misdemeanour – just the accumulation of lots of little things. Over a three-year period I'd been accumulating points on my licence, even while doing God's work. Maybe I'd be doing a family crisis appeal, with a car full of beds and clothing – but I'd be driving with one hand on the wheel and the other holding my phone. Once, I'd got lost trying to get to a service and turned right into a "no entry". Individually, they were trivial things, but collectively, enough to get me banned.

I rang Bruce and said, "Look, I'm in a mess. I'm depressed, I'm struggling, I'm overweight, I don't know where to turn. I don't want to be in church. I don't know if I'm meant to be in ministry. And if I'm not, what am I meant to be doing?"

He said, "You've just got to lay everything down, mate."

"Everything?"

"Everything."

That was in November 2017. For nearly five years I had been here, there, and everywhere, up and down the country, doing homeless feeds, homeless support, outreach, prison chaplaincy, sports chaplaincy, testimony, as well as handling family crises and being a father to my kids. I was like a hamster on a wheel doing a hundred miles an hour, and achieving nothing.

So, other than PinkLadies, which paid the bills, I dropped it all.

It did not come easy, of course. I was constantly feeling guilty. Should I be offering someone a bed? No, you've laid it down. Doing a homeless feed? No, you've laid that down too. But I had a wonderful Christmas at the end of 2017 – the first one where I was just at home with everyone I love. Everything else still happened without me.

In June 2018, we went on holiday as a family for the first time ever, to Mexico – my first holiday since I got out of prison, and my son Chris's first ever time on a plane. As it was taking off, the kids were on either side of me, clutching my arms and saying, "Thanks, Dad." And all the stress and worry and pain just drifted away.

For the first two days I kept checking my email and my social media, until finally I thought, "No, I need to switch off." We started to go places and have days out. We swam with dolphins. I was on a catamaran in the middle of the Caribbean, then snorkelling with my children either side of me, and I looked down through the mask at the seabed, and I just thought, "I used to beg on the streets of London."

I shared this story when we got back on the boat. As we went ashore, this young couple approached me. The man said, "I feel I need to tell you this – who you are and what you stand for has made this trip so worthwhile. I'm a born-again Christian too. We weren't going to come on this boat but we changed our minds, and you've really made this trip."

It turned out the rep on the site, Carlos, was also a born-again Christian. He had come from a biker gang. One of my pastor friends back home had been on a mission there and given me the address for a church, the closest one to my hotel, about a fifteen-minute drive. Carlos had been baptized in the sea in front of our hotel, and this was the church he went to. I attended, and there were thousands of people crying out to God. It seemed that wherever we went on that holiday, God placed somebody who was born again in front of me.

Chapter 26

THE GOOD, THE BAD, AND THE UGLY

The over-riding story of this book is transformational. A child, a judge, a cop, an offender, a mum or dad, an auntie – anyone can look at it and see that change is possible. Not wishy-washy easy – I've been as honest as I can about that – but possible. I'm a great believer that if we put everything out in the open – if we tell the truth and expose the stuff that normally people would hide – then, 1) it can't come back and bite us, and 2) that's truth.

I started this book with a wedding. I'd have liked it to have been my own… There's no sign of that yet. The closest I've come is the time I mistakenly identified my future wife, and told her so.

But then, *could* I have got married? Then, or even a year ago? My distorted view of love, sex, and relationships has taken a long, long time to unravel and get right. I think the fact that I've been single since becoming Christian has been part of that process, because all my relationships held a distorted view of love. The ability to love correctly would not be possible out of rejection, abandonment, bitterness, lack of discipline, lack of self-control, doing what I want. We've got to put the needs of other people before our own.

I used to look at Pat, my brother-in-law, as a no-mates geek because all he did was family life. But he was my biggest role model as a father figure. His character as a man, who loved my sister and his children so much and in so profound a way, means that they're still together after forty years of marriage. Providing for your family is love. Grounding your daughter because she's playing up is love. Telling your kids, "No, because that's bad for you" is love. It took a long time for me to get that, but it's the love that God has shown me in my Christian life, and that has enabled me to love others.

It's hard to submit to God when we see him as a punisher and not as a loving Father. I'd always had the view that he was beating me with a stick because I'd done wrong and he didn't like me. I wasn't seeing the fact that he chastises those he loves, and love has so many more dimensions than I thought.

I would dearly love to be married. I believe we're designed to live that way. To live single like Paul did, I think would need a special anointing. I think people who are OK with being on their own must have a special understanding.

But then I'm thinking, "When am I ever going to *meet* my wife?" I'm a single father and I work all week. I've been on Christian dating sites a couple of times, but I found I was just looking at the pictures. So then I changed tactic – I read the bio first, *then* looked at the pictures. Usually I would struggle with lust after that. Also, online dating is a very good way of ending up in bed after a couple of hours' acquaintance, so I don't do it any more.

The most important scripture that I stand on is from God himself: "It is not good for the man to be alone. I will make a helper suitable for him" (Genesis 2:18). I genuinely believe that the work that God is doing in me now, he's also doing in my wife, and then when we come together, it will be evident why we've both been through these processes. He is still healing the damage from other relationships, but I don't believe I'll be a singleton all my life. "Take delight in the Lord, and he will give you the desires of your heart" (Psalm 37:4).

The reality is that the longer I've been single, the more comfortable I am as a single man. The desire to be with somebody is not a sexual desire – it's deeper than that. It's for someone to share a life journey and my heart for the lost with. I would want my wife to be part of whatever ministry God has in mind for me, or at least be praying with me in it.

I have had an amazing ministry. I've ministered to people who can't have babies, and seen miracle births happen. I've been in prisons with the whole room coming forward and crying out to God in repentance. To receive a word of knowledge about a prisoner who's going to kill himself, and to give that word in a chapel service, and for that person to walk across the room, throw his arms around me, and just sob out his heart in front of everybody – that was a moment that I will never, ever forget. God has given me the ability to reach people that were unreachable. When significant things are happening like that, we need to be in a place where we can deal with it and handle it, because we are also going to come under attack. We come through a transforming experience all fired up for God, but it is so imperative that a period of process is allowed to happen. I wasn't allowing process to happen because I thought I knew better than everybody else. Since probably the first six months of my Christian life, which I now see as like a honeymoon period, my life has been under bombardment, mainly because I've stepped into levels of intensity that I'm just not meant to be taking on. If we are committed to reaching the lost, to binding up the broken-hearted, to prayer and fasting consistently, and everything else, then we're on the front line. Front-line soldiers get shot at, plain and simple.

So, if there are issues in our lives that are unresolved and undealt with, they've got to be exposed. Otherwise, the devil is just going to use them to trip us up.

Scripture talks about perseverance building character (Romans 5:4). I would give up and crumble, usually at the first hurdle. But somehow, I've just got an extra bit of fight as a Christian to persevere. In some scriptures it's called temperance – an old-fashioned word for self-control, for discipline. We must allow ourselves to be disciplined. God places people who are leaders and pastors and senior church members strategically, for his purposes and his plans. To allow somebody to speak into our lives and hold us accountable is paramount to the success of the Christian. And mark my words, if we do not allow that process to happen – if we step out from the God-given authority that some people have over us – then we will be sniped.

Being accountable, honest, open, humble, trusting – those are key things that are alien to people from my background. I didn't trust anybody, specifically men, and, as a career criminal, I had an anti-authority attitude anyway. So, the process can take time and may result in a good few wallopings along the way.

But failure is undervalued – I think we've got to get it wrong fifty times to get it right. If we don't get it wrong, we've got nothing to gauge from. People look at failure as final, but in fact it's the stepping board to success. Every major entrepreneur will have failed a hundred times. We succeed in our ability to get back up.

I could have made better choices. At seventeen I had the chance to be a professional. I could have reached a lot of people as a professional Rugby League player with a successful career. But rather than taking that route, I took another. Bruce and I shared the same choice at seventeen, chose differently, and lived different lives, but now we're both at the same place, side by side, reaching a lost community. Exactly the same story, but they're completely opposite poles.

I said earlier that not becoming a rent boy was just one of the times I genuinely believe the hand of God has been on my life. There was also the time as kids when we got on the wrong bus at a football game and we were going to get battered, but somehow we managed to avert it. Or when I managed to escape that kidnapping alive. There's the amount of drugs that I put into my body and never overdosed, when other people were overdosing left, right, and centre around me. My career as a cannabis grower that never got anywhere – either my crops died or the police raided. Getting onto heroin and off it again, in the space of a year. Relationships, friendships, the people that God's placed in my life, the great men that he's placed strategically when I didn't have a dad. It's all been a training ground. It's been my wilderness. My wilderness has been forty years of all that I've been through – the good, the bad, and the ugly to get me to this point.

The children of Israel were in the wilderness for forty years, and all that time the Promised Land was a fortnight's walk away. It's up to you how swiftly or how slowly you get there with your choices.

Chapter 27

A FAMILY AFFAIR

Deliverance has to be done in chunks and in stages. Right at the back end of 2017, I had to go through more of it, but beautifully this time with Bruce. Bruce had got the green light to establish his own church in Barnsley. Bentley Baptist was a huge part of my life and I'm very grateful for all that they did for me – but it felt right in January 2018 to move on and join Bruce in his new church. So, he has gone from mentor to pastor.

Then, for 2018, the year of laying everything down, I sought out a Christian counsellor who has helped me really fine-pick the residue. I talked over my memories of my mum. In chapter 22 I shared how David's prayer sessions began the healing process. It plugged a massive hole, and I was delivered from something – but it needed a working of the cross to follow up the deliverance.

I still couldn't get past the memory of my mum dead on the settee. Whenever I tried to picture her, that was all I got, which would trigger something and then my behaviour would spiral out of control. My new counsellor set me homework of putting my memories into boxes, one by one, and then working through them with people I trusted and prayed with – preferably men, because a lot of those memories would be men's stuff. I chose Bruce, and Pete, Bruce's pastor.

So we sat down and we prayed over this particular memory box. Pete asked where I thought my mum was now. And I remembered an out-of-body experience I once had as a child. I left my body – I was in the air, looking down at myself – and met with her. Together, we walked to the light, but suddenly I was told, "It's not your time." I had to return to my body. I always related that to heaven. It didn't seem like an evil, nasty, dark place. A lot of my past is a blurred fog, but I can see that, clear as a bell.

But my answer could only be the theologically correct one, as I understood it.

"She wasn't a believer, so she's in hell." I started to weep.

Pete said, "Did you love your mum?"

I said, "Yeah."

"So, do you think God loved her?" And then he told me about the two thieves crucified with Jesus. Salvation was offered to both of them. One received it and one didn't (Luke 23:39–43). As close as he could get to death, with the weight of the world sitting on his shoulders, Jesus offered salvation to those on their deathbed.

I saw that Jesus could have come to my mum at the end, as he did to the penitent thief – and if he did then all her bad things were washed away. She was forgiven. Those memories are not relevant – null and void. Everything I was holding against her has been nullified.

For more than twenty years I had focused on my pain and the negative aspects of our relationship. Suddenly, instead of that image of her on the settee, I saw a garden and a swing, and her as a small girl laughing. A pre-three-year-old, with a white dress on, just so happy.

Now, I saw the reality of my mum as a young, damaged girl, who lost her own mum when she was just three. Her grandfather beat her with a stick and her father abused her. Then came all the disastrous relationships I mentioned in chapter 2. She lost a child at birth.

I saw with new eyes that she was a strong-willed, hardworking woman whose life revolved around providing for her family. She was our rock and stability. Even though she was middle-aged, she did her best to provide for a hyperactive, boisterous boy who took a lot of handling. Everything she did revolved around me but I just threw it back, yearning for my dad, rubbing her face in it.

She was an old-school, roll-up-your-sleeves woman who was prepared to fight on our behalf. The violence I experienced from her had surely come from a place of sheer frustration, for there was never a time when I felt I wasn't loved. But my behaviour was off the wall. I had no respect and was spoiled both by her and by my two sisters. Then, when I was finally disciplined because she'd had enough, it was over the top.

I said that my mum died with a cigarette in her hand. It had burnt down to the filter. One little twitch or tremble, and that lit cigarette could have dropped and started a fire. We didn't have modern flame-retardant furniture. I could have died that night too. As my sister put it, they'd have been coming home to two dead bodies. I saw how Jesus had been acting even in that final moment of tragedy.

Clearing that blockage has helped me start to remember more good stuff, and has led to restoration with other family members too. I have a *wonderful* family, who have also been damaged and hurt. In fact, let's face it, my older siblings had it worse than I did – because they had me.

The best thing is that my mum will greet me in heaven. Instead of the falsehoods peddled by the spiritualists and mediums who claimed to be bringing her to me, we will be restored for eternity.

This wasn't the complete end of the story for my mum – more on that in the next chapter. But clearing that blockage has helped me start to remember more good stuff, and has – eventually – led to restoration with other family members too. That was a long haul.

Right back in chapter 1 I talked about meeting people that I hurt in my past. I've had grace and forgiveness from people I've assaulted and done serious harm to. But, thinking about it, even though those occasions were all extreme and violent, they were also one-offs. My family, on the other hand, I put through the mill over and over again, year after year after year. Time and again, as I grew up, I failed Rosemary, Pat, and Catherine, betraying all their trust in me. After them came my exes. First Bonnie, then Steph were trapped in volatile, hostile situations with a dangerous man who took drugs, and suffered mental health issues and paranoid delusions. They were at risk from my outbursts and from people associated with me coming round.

That was when I was with them. At other times, they were left with young children for years on end, by a guy who then wouldn't let go when he got back. I had a good way of targeting the people closest to them and intimidating them, to get at my exes. They and their families around them were rightly terrified.

At the time, I blamed them – in fact, I blamed everybody, circumstances, situations: anyone but myself. With Christian eyes, I see that I put them and their families through hell. I was a violent, drunken, drug-dealing wreck of a man. Even with the grace of God, you don't just get over that.

In Acts 9, the disciples don't exactly fall over themselves to accept their former persecutor Saul after his conversion. It takes personal testimony from Barnabas to bring them around. My family didn't have a Barnabas, and so it took them a *long* time to adjust to my new life. The shining example of the man I had become was a good argument, but it wasn't enough to cut through the scar tissue that I had inflicted on our relationships.

This may well be a problem that any new convert faces. You are full of the joy of your salvation – as far as you're concerned, you are a new creation, and so you're hurt when your loved ones just don't see it. They cling to their memories of the old you, and sometimes with good reason. Well, they too must go through processes of restoration with the new you.

In my case, it was prayer with my Christian counsellor, similar to the prayers that did away with the Hennessey heritage. We drew out my genealogy, prayed over it, and broke curses over it. Within a few weeks of that prayer, we all came together for a family photo shoot – and we got on. Five years after my conversion, my sister could finally look me in the face and say, "I know we've had issues in the past, but I want you to know how proud I am of what you've done within your life. I love you."

It was a hugely significant moment. God has restored that genealogy. She accepted me as a new man. It could only have come from me refusing to compromise my beliefs, and letting God work.

Then there was my dad. Just before this book went to the publisher, I finally had a real breakthrough with him too. It's harder to forgive someone who's still alive – they can still say and do things to hurt you. It had taken six years and I was still trying to forgive him. Eventually I realized that I simply couldn't do it... at least, in my own strength.

Instead, I had to ask God's forgiveness for my dad. I had to go to the cross and forgive as Jesus did: "Forgive him, Father, for he didn't know what he was doing." Finally, I gave God the opening to pour in the healing that he longed to give. As we prayed into those words from the cross, Pete put his hands on my shoulders, and looked me in the eyes, and said, "It is finished." He said it three times and I knew it was true. God forgave my father, so I could forgive him too.

Praise Jesus.

Chapter 28

IT IS FINISHED...?

I am a new creation. My relationships with my family have been restored. What more could I want?

Well...

In November 2014, while writing the first draft of this book – with no idea how much more work still lay ahead – I went on a weekend retreat in the heart of the Yorkshire Dales during which I had an amazing experience. There was a wooden cross on the hillside beside the outbuildings of the place – Scargill House, near Kettlewell – which intrigued me. I walked towards it, simply seeking guidance for the whole project, and when I started to pray, I had a sense of a brightness walking towards me, causing me to fall on my hands and face before the cross. "It is finished!" I heard the Lord say – the same words Pete would say about my dad, years later. The Lord was confirming that the book, my conversion, the whole of history, was all about the cross where he spoke those words: where love and mercy meet, where he paid the price of sin for all humanity, where he won the battle over the devil and all his hordes, and where he had set us free to live for him forever.

But when Jesus said "It is finished" on the cross, he meant it was finished for him but the start for us, humanity. We've won the war, but we might not win every battle. Jesus tells us, "Pick up your cross and follow me." It's a daily sacrifice. We're going to get it wrong; we're going to make mistakes. In the midst of all that, we need to keep our eyes focused on what was done at the cross.

And I know I am far from finished.

I took laying things down seriously, as per Bruce's advice. But for all that, 2018 was a wobbly year. For most of it, this book was my only project outside paid work. The interest from the publishers and finishing it off came at exactly the right time to fit in. But as the year went on, I began to feel troubled with the direction things were going in other areas. Opportunities arose to go into partnership with other ministries. There was the possibility of taking over a community building for an outreach project. Lots of different things were placed in my path, but I'd lost my sense of peace. It didn't help that even the regular paid work was diminishing. Issues arose in my family and in my finances that left me feeling disorientated. Then, in November, I took the big decision to move back to Barnsley. I was already going to Bruce's church there, but moving would bring me closer to my daughter's schooling. So, the reason for the move was sound – but on top of everything else, it inevitably made me feel even less settled.

It was while I was unpacking boxes that I felt the Lord saying, "I have to speak to you." It was a conversation I was desperate to have, and there is one place I have always been called to when that happens. Next morning, someone blessed me with a full tank of petrol and £100 worth of food money, so off I went to Ffald-y-Brenin.

It's not just your signal that fades as you approach Ffald-y-Brenin. The outside world recedes too. You lose contact and you gain clarity. This is when the Lord starts to prepare your heart. In this case, he told me very clearly, "I need to speak to you about your mum."

That threw me – "Lord, we've dealt with that! Twice!" First with David Augur, then with Bruce and Pete. I wasn't sure what else needed doing. Still, that was the message, so I pressed on to see what God had in store.

You might think you've heard this before, but I got there and there was no room... That wasn't a concern. I just wanted to be there. They said, "Do you want to look at a B&B?" That would have taken me off site, and I felt that here was where I was meant to be, so I said no.

I went out to the high cross and shouted out my frustration to the Lord. I had that £100 on me. I said, "I'm meant to be here, Lord, no matter what. So I'm going to pay for a couple of nights and ask you to bless this ministry, whether I stay or not."

I went down to reception to pay. "Oh," they said, "a room has appeared."

A group of women had arrived on retreat together. One of them hadn't come, so the room was free, though they had to ask the ladies if they minded a man being placed among them. They had no objection, and in the time we were together I washed up for them and generally helped out.

We also sat in silence for an hour in a prayer meeting, and at the end one of them said, "I've got a word for Allen." I waited, expectant. "Don't get burned out."

Burned out. That exactly described how I was feeling. Drained, lethargic, putting weight on again, struggling to get through the days.

The ladies left before I did. As a parting gift they gave me Brother Lawrence's *The Practice of the Presence of God*, and asked if they could pray. They prayed that the Lord would place mothers around me at strategic points; that he would bless me in the prayers and love of mothers. God was keeping the mother theme fresh in my mind. One said I had a unique anointing – a unique ministry. I was going to reach people from different backgrounds in a revolutionary way. Another said I was a bit of a wild man – not referring to my past, but to my future. I was not going to be fitting into a regular, conforming pattern. Whatever the ministry the Lord had in mind for me turned out to be, it was going to be... wild!

The ladies left on Sunday. That was the second night I had paid for. I was meant to be going home the next morning, on Monday, but when I woke up, I just knew in myself that it wasn't time to go. I had work scheduled back home, so I went up the hill to get some signal – the only place you can at Ffald-y-Brenin – and cleared my diary for a week. I'd struggled for so long. I *had* to have this week to get some peace and focus, otherwise I would just burn out – and I had been specifically told not to do that!

Then it was time for morning prayer, and to tell the leaders I wasn't ready to go. The same thing happened again: my booking was up so there was no room. They juggled the books as best they could to see if they could accommodate me; and then someone didn't turn up, so I could stay until Wednesday.

Over the next couple of days, I did a lot of reading: my Brother Lawrence book, from the ladies, and *The Shack*. I shared my heart and how I felt with a lot of people. I went into the chapel to pray for God's peace. The theme of my prayer has always been for anointing: "Lord, I pray for anointing to do your work and your will in..." followed by whatever was on my mind at the time. I supposed I had come to Ffald-y-Brenin for anointing in whatever I was meant to be doing – and discernment to learn what that was.

And on the Tuesday, my last full day at Ffald-y-Brenin, it came to me. My disquiet was because I was still involved in stuff that wasn't meant for me. I thought I was keeping my options open for whatever God had in mind for me – but I was still looking back. I had reached the end of a chapter and I wanted the old chapter to keep going as before.

In fact, this is a new chapter. A new season for me. All the things that bothered me belonged to the last chapter. I had to let them go.

Yes, I needed anointing. I needed the anointing of God to go forward into that next stage of my life. The life that the ladies had been looking ahead to in their prophecies. What does that life hold? As of now – I have absolutely no idea. It should be terrifying. It isn't.

It was a breakthrough. Part of the disquiet that had brought me to Ffald-y-Brenin was that stuff just kept going off in my mind, and as soon as I tried to concentrate on one thing, off my mind went in a new direction. I was struggling to retain peace. But, for the rest of that day, as troubles came at me in my head, I just gave them to God, gave them to God, gave them to God, over and again.

As I went to bed, Ffald-y-Brenin was hit by a ravaging storm. The next day, several people said they had had a broken night as the storm kept them awake. I had barely noticed it. I was reading the book of Acts, including chapter 27 where Paul is kept safe in the heart of the storm. I'd been in the eye of the storm for most of 2018. Now I had a stillness in my heart. It doesn't matter what's going off, God said – just be still.

And also that night, I read the publisher's draft of this book, from beginning to end. I had never been completely happy with it and I finally I realized why. Like my thinking, it was still based in my old life. It ended with a vague assumption that God would continue his good works in me, as before. In fact, this book should mark the end of the old chapter altogether. The publishers kindly let me alter the ending to the one you're now reading. This is not a new chapter in this story – it is the start of the next one.

The next morning, as it always does, my phone pinged with a scripture for the day. 2 Corinthians 12:9: "My grace is sufficient for you, for my power is made perfect in weakness." It was the final confirmation. God is still glorified, even if I am a work in progress.

It was the day to leave, and this time I felt ready to do so. But God still had surprises in store for me. For a start, he hadn't really addressed the thing he had told me about as I had driven into the valley – my mum.

I went down to the morning service and it was packed. Ffald-y-Brenin has intercessors from all around the world who pray for it, and they were all there for a conference. We shared a beautiful time with the Lord for an hour. As the prayers came to an end, people began shouting out the names of the nations where they were from. "Canada!" "India!" And my ears pricked up as I heard someone say, "Israel!"

Israel has been on my heart for a long time. I have come to see the importance of Israel in God's overall plan.

When I was listening to one of Derek Prince's talks, "Why Israel?", I was so convicted that I had to pull over and repent on behalf of myself, my ancestors, and of Great Britain for the disgraceful way we had treated God's Chosen People. Britain was meant to be built on Christian values, and my heart was stirred to hear the atrocities our forefathers had committed – not least signing away their land at the stroke of a pen.

We are already seeing the fulfilment of one of the key prophecies indicating the imminent return of Christ – of Jews migrating to the Promised Land from every corner of the globe. And the Bible pronounces a blessing on those who bless Israel (Genesis 12:2–3; Numbers 24:9). I often drive through the Manchester suburb of Prestwich on my way to my Christian counselling, and Prestwich has a large Jewish community. I always hope I will be able to offer a lift to a Jew, or help out in some way, to receive that blessing!

So, I was very interested to meet this person from Israel. She turned out to be an American lady, a Messianic Jew from California, who had moved to Israel six years earlier. There was a group of ladies with her. (See how God continues to bless me through women?) I told her I wanted to give them a blessing – and she said exactly the same thing. "Would you sit down? I want to give you an Israeli blessing."

She did. She prayed over me in Hebrew and English. She anointed me with oil from the Mount of Olives, and marked my head with a cross. Echoing the prayers of two days earlier, she and her friends prophesied supernatural healings over me; that people would come from all over to hear me; that there was a power of healing in me she had never seen before. I began to feel agitated – people were saying things I didn't know about myself. I hadn't looked for this at all – I had wanted to bless them!

And then a sweet old lady – I don't know how old, but her great-grandchildren are pastors – prayed the most amazing prayer with me.

First, she asked if she could touch me. She laid her hands on me and spoke in a quiet, American purr, with a soft determination that could not be denied.

> *Father, you have put many desires in his*
> *heart... So we call them forth in the name of*
> *Jesus... Lord, you have given him a mouth*
> *to speak your oracles... I pray that he will*
> *glorify your name in such a way in this season*
> *that it will be an amazement to him and an*
> *amazement to others... that when he touches*
> *the broken, when he ministers to the diseases*
> *of others, that he will see your purpose and*
> *your plan completed within them; that the*
> *lame would walk, the blind would see... He*
> *has looked at crippled people and he has said,*
> *"O God, why don't they walk?" Would you give*
> *him the courage to lay his hand and call forth*

their wholeness, and we will give you the praise
and the glory for it…

Finally, she asked if she could kiss me on the cheek, and she went on with the most amazing gentleness.

I'm going to kiss you on the cheek, is that all
right? As a mum, I kiss you. As a mum, I love
you. As a mum, I heal that broken heart in you
in Jesus' name. Go in the power and strength of
the Holy Spirit, son.

This woman was a complete stranger, yet she reached out to me as a mum and she called me "son". She had no inkling about me, the journey I'd been on, or the importance of my mum. As she prayed over me, I was speaking in tongues that felt different to any I'd spoken in before, and I was weeping.

God has done something with a purpose and a plan. I believe I have now been anointed to follow that purpose.

After the Israeli blessing, a lady of Native American ancestry gave me a Native American blessing. Somehow in the past her tribe had intermarried with the Mountbatten family, so she blessed me on their behalf too. And just as I left Ffald-y-Brenin, the staff gave me a blessing of their own. So I left with an Israeli blessing, a Native American blessing, an English gentry blessing and a Welsh blessing all ringing in my ears, with prophecies of blind eyes opening, the paralysed getting up, diseases being healed.

And, healing of my own! I finally realized what God had meant about my mum. That amazing prayer was the final stage. David Augur had put a plug in a big hole, and Bruce and Pete had cleared out the residue. But this was the final balm of healing, spread over the wound. The Lord's final deliverance from the pain and trauma of my mum. The last thing that could hold me back from ... whatever God has in mind.

Both the other times I'd been to Ffald-y-Brenin, it had been with an agenda. I knew exactly what I wanted; God then did something completely different. This time I got what I wanted but it was through means I could never have expected. This is the end of this journey, before the next journey that the Lord will now take me on. I've been asking for anointing, and I've been anointed.

* * *

I still go back to Cusworth Hall, to sit on my favourite seat and look out over Doncaster. The place where I used to play truant and fight and wee on my friends has been reclaimed as the place I pray.

I often go for a drive around Scawsby. It helps me reconnect with my roots and keeps the amazing journey that I've been on, the things that God has done for me, fresh in my mind. These were the places that shaped me. God is shaping me still. I don't fit into any particular box.

So, is it finished? Not by a long shot.

I will wait on what the Lord has in mind, and meanwhile, I'm still the guy who has coffee with policemen and hugs judges.

EPILOGUE

Well, that's my life so far! You can read it. You're holding it in your hands. You've seen rags to riches and riches to rags, many times over. The mistakes, the weaknesses, the problems. Sometimes you must have wondered if there was any way out of it.

There was, and there is, for the very simple reason that his grace is sufficient. Never lose sight of that. Never forget it. However bad your own situation, Christ can redeem it. You can see how bad a man I was, and I'll be the first to say now that I'm still a work in progress – don't think that this is all. But one thing I can say for certain, beyond any shadow of a doubt, is that I am one hundred per cent, entirely and completely saved by Jesus, who makes all things new. *All* things. There is *hope* in Jesus Christ: hope, freedom, and a future for you. He is the starting point of the rest of your life, and he's only a prayer away.

Seriously, guys, anything is possible. I can't say it often enough. I have travelled on an incredible journey – from crying on my knees in prison to sitting in a rugby stand with a Police Commissioner and the Shadow Home Secretary. How else could this possibly have happened?

Would you like to know this for yourself? The first step is always repentance. Jesus loves you more than you can ever know – but he also loves you so much that he will never force himself on you. He will abide by your choices, even though it breaks his heart. So, you must turn away from your old life. Even if, like me, you find yourself turning straight back again, the act of repentance gives Jesus a way into your life – and he will not let you go after that.

If you're not sure where to start, may I invite you to say this prayer with me? This is the prayer I lead the prisoners in, and it encapsulates the gospel message:

Dear God

I know that I am a sinner, and I ask your forgiveness. I know that when Jesus Christ died on the cross, he paid the penalty for my sins. At this moment, I commit myself to turning from sin and accepting Jesus Christ as my personal Saviour and Lord. Send upon me your Holy Spirit to fill me, guide me, and help me to become the sort of person you want me to be. Thank you for loving me, Father. In Jesus' name.

Amen

Then follow it through by seeking out mature Christians, as I have done. If you have just said this prayer, I look forward to welcoming you into a new and exciting life!